MznLnx

Missing Links Exam Preps

Exam Prep for

College Algebra with Modeling and Visualization

Rockswold, 3rd Edition

The MznLnx Exam Prep is your link from the texbook and lecture to your exams.
The MznLnx Exam Preps are unauthorized and comprehensive reviews of your textbooks.

All material provided by MznLnx and Rico Publications (c) 2010
Textbook publishers and textbook authors do not particpate in or contribute to these reviews.

MznLnx

Rico
Publications

Exam Prep for College Algebra with Modeling and Visualization
3rd Edition
Rockswold

Publisher: Raymond Houge
Assistant Editor: Michael Rouger
Text and Cover Designer: Lisa Buckner
Marketing Manager: Sara Swagger
Project Manager, Editorial Production: Jerry Emerson
Art Director: Vernon Lowerui

Product Manager: Dave Mason
Editorial Assitant: Rachel Guzmanji
Pedagogy: Debra Long
Cover Image: Jim Reed/Getty Images
Text and Cover Printer: City Printing, Inc.
Compositor: Media Mix, Inc.

(c) 2010 Rico Publications
ALL RIGHTS RESERVED. No part of this work covered by the copyright may be reproduced or used in any form or by an means--graphic, electronic, or mechanical, including photocopying, recording, taping, Web distribution, information storage, and retrieval systems, or in any other manner--without the written permission of the publisher.

Printed in the United States
ISBN:

For more information about our products, contact us at:
Dave.Mason@RicoPublications.com

For permission to use material from this text or product, submit a request online to:
Dave.Mason@RicoPublications.com

Contents

CHAPTER 1
Introduction To Functions and Graphs — 1

CHAPTER 2
Linear Functions and Equations — 20

CHAPTER 3
Quadratic Functions and Equations — 40

CHAPTER 4
Nonlinear Functions and Equations — 55

CHAPTER 5
Exponential and Logarithmic Functions — 77

CHAPTER 6
Systems of Equations and Inequalities — 99

CHAPTER 7
Conic Sections — 122

CHAPTER 8
Further Topics in Algebra — 132

ANSWER KEY — 159

TO THE STUDENT

COMPREHENSIVE

The *MznLnx* Exam Prep series is designed to help you pass your exams. Editors at MznLnx review your textbooks and then prepare these practice exams to help you master the textbook material. Unlike study guides, workbooks, and practice tests provided by the texbook publisher and textbook authors, *MznLnx* gives you **all** of the material in each chapter in exam form, not just samples, so you can be sure to nail your exam.

MECHANICAL

The MznLnx Exam Prep series creates exams that will help you learn the subject matter as well as test you on your understanding. Each question is designed to help you master the concept. Just working through the exams, you gain an understanding of the subject--its a simple mechanical process that produces success.

INTEGRATED STUDY GUIDE AND REVIEW

MznLnx is not just a set of exams designed to test you, its also a comprehensive review of the subject content. Each exam question is also a review of the concept, making sure that you will get the answer correct without having to go to other sources of material. You learn as you go! Its the easiest way to pass an exam.

HUMOR

Studying can be tedious and dry. MznLnx's instructional design includes moderate humor within the exam questions on occassion, to break the tedium and revitalize the brain

Chapter 1. Introduction To Functions and Graphs

1. In mathematics, a _____ can mean either an element of the set {1, 2, 3, ...} (i.e the positive integers or the counting numbers) or an element of the set {0, 1, 2, 3, ...} (i.e. the non-negative integers).
   - a. Thing
   - b. Natural number0
   - c. Undefined
   - d. Undefined

2. Mathematical _____ is used to represent ideas.
   - a. Thing
   - b. Notation0
   - c. Undefined
   - d. Undefined

3. _____ is a synonym for information.
   - a. Data0
   - b. Thing
   - c. Undefined
   - d. Undefined

4. _____ is a notation for writing numbers that is often used by scientists and mathematicians to make it easier to write large and small numbers.
   - a. Thing
   - b. Scientific notation0
   - c. Undefined
   - d. Undefined

5. A _____ is a symbol or group of symbols, or a word in a natural language that represents a number.
   - a. Thing
   - b. Numeral0
   - c. Undefined
   - d. Undefined

6. _____ numerals are a numeral system originating in ancient Rome, adapted from Etruscan numerals.
   - a. Thing
   - b. Roman0
   - c. Undefined
   - d. Undefined

7. _____ is a set of numbers, in the broadest sense of the word, together with one or more operations, such as addition or multiplication.
   - a. Number system0
   - b. Thing
   - c. Undefined
   - d. Undefined

8. A _____ is a number that is less than zero.
   - a. Negative number0
   - b. Thing
   - c. Undefined
   - d. Undefined

9. _____ element of an element x with respect to a binary operation * with identity element e is an element y such that x * y = y * x = e. In particular,
   - a. Thing
   - b. Inverse0
   - c. Undefined
   - d. Undefined

10. In mathematics, the _____ inverse, or opposite, of a number n is the number that, when added to n, yields zero. The _____ inverse of n is denoted −n.
    - a. Thing
    - b. Additive0
    - c. Undefined
    - d. Undefined

11. In mathematics, the _____ of a number n is the number that, when added to n, yields zero. The _____ of n is denoted −n. For example, 7 is −7, because 7 + (−7) = 0, and the _____ of −0.3 is 0.3, because −0.3 + 0.3 = 0.

Chapter 1. Introduction To Functions and Graphs

    a. Additive inverse0   b. Thing
    c. Undefined   d. Undefined

12. In banking and accountancy, the outstanding _____ is the amount of money owned, or due, that remains in a deposit account or a loan account at a given date, after all past remittances, payments and withdrawal have been accounted for.
    a. Thing   b. Balance0
    c. Undefined   d. Undefined

13. A _____ is a quantity that denotes the proportional amount or magnitude of one quantity relative to another.
    a. Ratio0   b. Thing
    c. Undefined   d. Undefined

14. In mathematics, a _____ number is a number which can be expressed as a ratio of two integers. Non-integer _____ numbers (commonly called fractions) are usually written as the vulgar fraction a / b, where b is not zero.
    a. Thing   b. Rational0
    c. Undefined   d. Undefined

15. The _____ are the only integral domain whose positive elements are well-ordered, and in which order is preserved by addition. Like the natural numbers, the _____ form a countably infinite set. The set of all _____ is usually denoted in mathematics by a boldface Z .
    a. Integers0   b. Thing
    c. Undefined   d. Undefined

16. Equivalence is the condition of being _____ or essentially equal.
    a. Equivalent0   b. Thing
    c. Undefined   d. Undefined

17. In mathematics, a _____ may be described informally as a number that can be given by an infinite decimal representation.
    a. Thing   b. Real number0
    c. Undefined   d. Undefined

18. A _____ decimal is a decimal fraction which ends after a definite number of digits.
    a. Terminating0   b. Thing
    c. Undefined   d. Undefined

19. In mathematics, an _____ number is any real number that is not a rational number- that is, it is a number which cannot be expressed as a fraction m/n, where m and n are integers.
    a. Thing   b. Irrational0
    c. Undefined   d. Undefined

20. In mathematics, an _____ is any real number that is not a rational number ¡ª that is, it is a number which cannot be expressed as m/n, where m and n are integers.

Chapter 1. Introduction To Functions and Graphs

a. Irrational number0
b. Thing
c. Undefined
d. Undefined

21. In mathematics, _____ are any real number that is not a rational number ¡ª that is, it is a number which cannot be expressed as m/n, where m and n are integers.
    a. Thing
    b. Irrational numbers0
    c. Undefined
    d. Undefined

22. In mathematics, an _____, mean, or central tendency of a data set refers to a measure of the "middle" or "expected" value of the data set.
    a. Average0
    b. Concept
    c. Undefined
    d. Undefined

23. The _____, the average in everyday English, which is also called the arithmetic _____ (and is distinguished from the geometric _____ or harmonic _____). The average is also called the sample _____. The expected value of a random variable, which is also called the population _____.
    a. Mean0
    b. Thing
    c. Undefined
    d. Undefined

24. A _____ is the result of the addition of a set of numbers. The numbers may be natural numbers, complex numbers, matrices, or still more complicated objects. An infinite _____ is a subtle procedure known as a series.
    a. Sum0
    b. Thing
    c. Undefined
    d. Undefined

25. In business, particularly accounting, a _____ is the time intervals that the accounts, statement, payments, or other calculations cover.
    a. Period0
    b. Thing
    c. Undefined
    d. Undefined

26. _____ refers to all non-domesticated plants, animals, and other organisms.
    a. Thing
    b. Wildlife0
    c. Undefined
    d. Undefined

27. A _____ is an individual or household that purchases and uses goods and services generated within the economy.
    a. Consumer0
    b. Thing
    c. Undefined
    d. Undefined

28. _____ is a statistical time-series measure of a weighted average of prices of a specified set of goods and services purchased by consumers
    a. Consumer price index0
    b. Thing
    c. Undefined
    d. Undefined

29. A _____ is a special kind of ratio, indicating a relationship between two measurements with different units, such as miles to gallons or cents to pounds.

a. Thing
b. Rate0
c. Undefined
d. Undefined

30. The word _____ is used in a variety of ways in mathematics.
a. Thing
b. Index0
c. Undefined
d. Undefined

31. In mainstream economics, the word _____ refers to a general rise in prices measured against a standard level of purchasing power.
a. Thing
b. Inflation0
c. Undefined
d. Undefined

32. A _____ is a function that assigns a number to subsets of a given set.
a. Measure0
b. Thing
c. Undefined
d. Undefined

33. _____ is the fee paid on borrowed money.
a. Thing
b. Interest0
c. Undefined
d. Undefined

34. In Euclidean geometry, a uniform _____ is a linear transformation that enlargers or diminishes objects, and whose _____ factor is the same in all directions. This is also called homothety.
a. Thing
b. Scale0
c. Undefined
d. Undefined

35. An _____ is the fee paid on borrow money.
a. Interest rate0
b. Concept
c. Undefined
d. Undefined

36. _____ is a way of expressing a number as a fraction of 100 per cent meaning "per hundred".
a. Thing
b. Percent0
c. Undefined
d. Undefined

37. In mathematics, a _____ or rhodonea curve is a sinusoid plotted in polar coordinates.
a. Thing
b. Rose0
c. Undefined
d. Undefined

38. In mathematics, the _____ (or modulus) of a real number is its numerical value without regard to its sign.
a. Absolute value0
b. Thing
c. Undefined
d. Undefined

39. An _____ is a combination of numbers, operators, grouping symbols and/or free variables and bound variables arranged in a meaningful way which can be evaluated..
a. Thing
b. Expression0
c. Undefined
d. Undefined

Chapter 1. Introduction To Functions and Graphs

40. _____ is a mathematical operation, written a^n, involving two numbers, the base a and the exponent n.
    a. Exponentiating0   b. Thing
    c. Undefined   d. Undefined

41. _____ is a mathematical operation, written a^n, involving two numbers, the base a and the exponent n.
    a. Exponentiation0   b. Thing
    c. Undefined   d. Undefined

42. _____ is a branch of mathematics concerning the study of structure, relation and quantity.
    a. Concept   b. Algebra0
    c. Undefined   d. Undefined

43. _____ has many meanings, most of which simply .
    a. Power0   b. Thing
    c. Undefined   d. Undefined

44. The _____ is a property of multiplication or addition where the product or sum remains the same, regardless of whether or not the order of the addends or factors are changed.
    a. Thing   b. Commutative property0
    c. Undefined   d. Undefined

45. A _____ is a three-dimensional solid object bounded by six square faces, facets, or sides, with three meeting at each vertex.
    a. Cube0   b. Thing
    c. Undefined   d. Undefined

46. A _____ of a number is a number a such that a^3 = x.
    a. Cube root0   b. Thing
    c. Undefined   d. Undefined

47. In mathematics, a _____ of a complex-valued function f is a member x of the domain of f such that f(x) vanishes at x, that is, x : f (x) = 0.
    a. Thing   b. Root0
    c. Undefined   d. Undefined

48. In plane geometry, a _____ is a polygon with four equal sides, four right angles, and parallel opposite sides. In algebra, the _____ of a number is that number multiplied by itself.
    a. Thing   b. Square0
    c. Undefined   d. Undefined

49. In mathematics, a _____ of a number x is a number r such that r^2 = x, or in words, a number r whose square (the result of multiplying the number by itself) is x.
    a. Square root0   b. Thing
    c. Undefined   d. Undefined

Chapter 1. Introduction To Functions and Graphs

50. _____ is a set, with some particular properties and usually some additional structure, such as the operations of addition or multiplication, for instance.
   a. Space0
   b. Thing
   c. Undefined
   d. Undefined

51. _____ is a kind of property which exists as magnitude or multitude. It is among the basic classes of things along with quality, substance, change, and relation.
   a. Amount0
   b. Thing
   c. Undefined
   d. Undefined

52. Multiple Signal Classification, also known as _____, is an algorithm used for frequency estimation and emitter location.
   a. Thing
   b. Music0
   c. Undefined
   d. Undefined

53. The decimal separator is a symbol used to mark the boundary between the integral and the fractional parts of a decimal numeral. Terms implying the symbol used are _____ and decimal comma.
   a. Decimal point0
   b. Concept
   c. Undefined
   d. Undefined

54. _____ forms part of thinking. Considered the most complex of all intellectual functions, _____ has been defined as higher-order cognitive process that requires the modulation and control of more routine or fundamental skills.
   a. Problem solving0
   b. Thing
   c. Undefined
   d. Undefined

55. _____ is the transport of people on a trip/journey or the process or time involved in a person or object moving from one location to another.
   a. Travel0
   b. Thing
   c. Undefined
   d. Undefined

56. In classical geometry, a _____ of a circle or sphere is any line segment from its center to its boundary. By extension, the _____ of a circle or sphere is the length of any such segment. The _____ is half the diameter. In science and engineering the term _____ of curvature is commonly used as a synonym for _____.
   a. Radius0
   b. Thing
   c. Undefined
   d. Undefined

57. In physics, an _____ is the path that an object makes around another object while under the influence of a source of centripetal force, such as gravity.
   a. Orbit0
   b. Thing
   c. Undefined
   d. Undefined

58. A _____ is a unit of length, usually used to measure distance, in a number of different systems, including Imperial units, United States customary units and Norwegian/Swedish mil. Its size can vary from system to system, but in each is between 1 and 10 kilometers. In contemporary English contexts _____ refers to either:

Chapter 1. Introduction To Functions and Graphs

    a. Thing
    b. Mile0
    c. Undefined
    d. Undefined

59. _____ is a unit of speed, expressing the number of international miles covered per hour.
    a. Thing
    b. Miles per hour0
    c. Undefined
    d. Undefined

60. In Euclidean geometry, a _____ is the set of all points in a plane at a fixed distance, called the radius, from a given point, the center.
    a. Circle0
    b. Thing
    c. Undefined
    d. Undefined

61. The _____ is the distance around a closed curve. _____ is a kind of perimeter.
    a. Thing
    b. Circumference0
    c. Undefined
    d. Undefined

62. The _____ of a solid object is the three-dimensional concept of how much space it occupies, often quantified numerically.
    a. Volume0
    b. Thing
    c. Undefined
    d. Undefined

63. _____ is the distance around a given two-dimensional object. As a general rule, the _____ of a polygon can always be calculated by adding all the length of the sides together. So, the formula for triangles is P = a + b + c, where a, b and c stand for each side of it. For quadrilaterals the equation is P = a + b + c + d. For equilateral polygons, P = na, where n is the number of sides and a is the side length.
    a. Thing
    b. Perimeter0
    c. Undefined
    d. Undefined

64. In mathematics, a _____ is a quadric surface, with the following equation in Cartesian coordinates: $(x/a)^2 + (y/b)^2 = 1$.
    a. Thing
    b. Cylinder0
    c. Undefined
    d. Undefined

65. _____ is the estimation of a physical quantity such as distance, energy, temperature, or time.
    a. Thing
    b. Measurement0
    c. Undefined
    d. Undefined

66. In mathematics and logic, a _____ proof is a way of showing the truth or falsehood of a given statement by a straightforward combination of established facts, usually existing lemmas and theorems, without making any further assumptions.
    a. Thing
    b. Direct0
    c. Undefined
    d. Undefined

67. _____ is an adjective usually refering to being in the centre.

a. Thing
b. Central0
c. Undefined
d. Undefined

68. _____ is a physical property of a system that underlies the common notions of hot and cold; something that is hotter has the greater _____.
   a. Thing
   b. Temperature0
   c. Undefined
   d. Undefined

69. U.S. liquid _____ is legally defined as 231 cubic inches, and is equal to 3.785411784 litres or abotu 0.13368 cubic feet. This is the most common definition of a _____. The U.S. fluid ounce is defined as 1/128 of a U.S. _____.
   a. Thing
   b. Gallon0
   c. Undefined
   d. Undefined

70. _____ is a term applied when talking about the movement of air from one place to the next.
   a. Thing
   b. Wind speed0
   c. Undefined
   d. Undefined

71. The metre (or _____, see spelling differences) is a measure of length. It is the basic unit of length in the metric system and in the International System of Units (SI), used around the world for general and scientific purposes.
   a. Meter0
   b. Concept
   c. Undefined
   d. Undefined

72. A _____ is a compensation which workers receive in exchange for their labor.
   a. Wage0
   b. Thing
   c. Undefined
   d. Undefined

73. A _____, as defined by the International Astronomical Union, is a celestial body orbiting a star or stellar remnant that is massive enough to be rounded by its own gravity, not massive enough to cause thermonuclear fusion in its core, and has cleared its neighboring region of planetesimals.
   a. Planet0
   b. Thing
   c. Undefined
   d. Undefined

74. The _____ in a vacuum is an important physical constant denoted by the letter c for constant or the Latin word celeritas meaning "swiftness
   a. Speed of light0
   b. Thing
   c. Undefined
   d. Undefined

75. _____ is electromagnetic radiation with a wavelength that is visible to the eye (visible _____) or, in a technical or scientific context, electromagnetic radiation of any wavelength.
   a. Thing
   b. Light0
   c. Undefined
   d. Undefined

Chapter 1. Introduction To Functions and Graphs

76. In geometry, a _____ (Greek words diairo = divide and metro = measure) of a circle is any straight line segment that passes through the centre and whose endpoints are on the circular boundary, or, in more modern usage, the length of such a line segment. When using the word in the more modern sense, one speaks of the _____ rather than a _____, because all diameters of a circle have the same length. This length is twice the radius. The _____ of a circle is also the longest chord that the circle has.
    a. Thing
    b. Diameter0
    c. Undefined
    d. Undefined

77. In sociology and biology a _____ is the collection of people or organisms of a particular species living in a given geographic area or space, usually measured by a census.
    a. Population0
    b. Thing
    c. Undefined
    d. Undefined

78. _____ is the property of a physical object that quantifies the amount of matter and energy it is equivalent to.
    a. Mass0
    b. Thing
    c. Undefined
    d. Undefined

79. In mathematics, a _____ function in the sense of algebraic geometry is an everywhere-defined, polynomial function on an algebraic variety V with values in the field K over which V is defined.
    a. Regular0
    b. Thing
    c. Undefined
    d. Undefined

80. In a mathematical proof or a syllogism, a _____ is a statement that is the logical consequence of preceding statements.
    a. Conclusion0
    b. Concept
    c. Undefined
    d. Undefined

81. Acid _____ ratio measures the ability of a company to use its near cash or quick assets to immediately extinguish its current liabilities.
    a. Thing
    b. Test0
    c. Undefined
    d. Undefined

82. A _____ is a one-dimensional picture in which the integers are shown as specially-marked points evenly spaced on a line.
    a. Thing
    b. Number line0
    c. Undefined
    d. Undefined

83. Deductive _____ is the kind of _____ in which the conclusion is necessitated by, or reached from, previously known facts (the premises).
    a. Reasoning0
    b. Thing
    c. Undefined
    d. Undefined

84. In probability theory and statistics, a _____ is a number dividing the higher half of a sample, a population, or a probability distribution from the lower half.

a. Median0
b. Concept
c. Undefined
d. Undefined

85. In mathematics, the _____ of a function is the set of all "output" values produced by that function. Given a function $f : A \to B$, the _____ of f, is defined to be the set $\{x \in B : x = f(a) \text{ for some } a \in A\}$.
    a. Thing
    b. Range0
    c. Undefined
    d. Undefined

86. In mathematics, a statistical _____ of a set of data is a measure how observations in the data set are distributed across various categories.
    a. Dispersion0
    b. Thing
    c. Undefined
    d. Undefined

87. An _____ is a collection of two not necessarily distinct objects, one of which is distinguished as the first coordinate and the other as the second coordinate.
    a. Thing
    b. Ordered pair0
    c. Undefined
    d. Undefined

88. In mathematics, the conjugate _____ or adjoint matrix of an m-by-n matrix A with complex entries is the n-by-m matrix A* obtained from A by taking the transpose and then taking the complex conjugate of each entry.
    a. Thing
    b. Pairs0
    c. Undefined
    d. Undefined

89. In mathematics, a _____ of a k-place relation $L \subseteq X_1 \times \ldots \times X_k$ is one of the sets X_j, $1 \leq j \leq k$. In the special case where k = 2 and $L \subseteq X_1 \times X_2$ is a function $L : X_1 \to X_2$, it is conventional to refer to X_1 as the _____ of the function and to refer to X_2 as the codomain of the function.
    a. Thing
    b. Domain0
    c. Undefined
    d. Undefined

90. A _____ is a set of numbers that designate location in a given reference system, such as x,y in a planar _____ system or an x,y,z in a three-dimensional _____ system.
    a. Thing
    b. Coordinate0
    c. Undefined
    d. Undefined

91. In mathematics, a _____ is a two-dimensional manifold or surface that is perfectly flat.
    a. Plane0
    b. Thing
    c. Undefined
    d. Undefined

92. _____ means of or relating to the French philosopher and mathematician René Descartes.
    a. Cartesian0
    b. Thing
    c. Undefined
    d. Undefined

93. An _____ is a straight line around which a geometric figure can be rotated.
    a. Thing
    b. Axis0
    c. Undefined
    d. Undefined

Chapter 1. Introduction To Functions and Graphs   11

94. In astronomy, geography, geometry and related sciences and contexts, a plane is said to be _____ at a given point if it is locally perpendicular to the gradient of the gravity field, i.e., with the direction of the gravitational force at that point.
   a. Thing
   b. Horizontal0
   c. Undefined
   d. Undefined

95. A _____ consists of one quarter of the coordinate plane.
   a. Quadrant0
   b. Thing
   c. Undefined
   d. Undefined

96. An _____ or member of a set is an object that when collected together make up the set.
   a. Element0
   b. Thing
   c. Undefined
   d. Undefined

97. In mathematics, the _____ , or members of a set or more generally a class are all those objects which when collected together make up the set or class.
   a. Thing
   b. Elements0
   c. Undefined
   d. Undefined

98. A _____, scatter diagram or scatter graph is a graph used in statistics to visually display and relate two quantitative variables of a multidimensional data set by displaying the data as a collection of points, each having one coordinate on a horizontal and one on a vertical axis.
   a. Thing
   b. Scatterplot0
   c. Undefined
   d. Undefined

99. In geometry, a line _____ is a part of a line that is bounded by two end points, and contains every point on the line between its end points.
   a. Concept
   b. Segment0
   c. Undefined
   d. Undefined

100. _____ is often used to describe the measurement of the steepness, incline, gradient, or grade of a straight line. The _____ is defined as the ratio of the "rise" divided by the "run" between two points on a line, or in other words, the ratio of the altitude change to the horizontal distance between any two points on the line.
   a. Slope0
   b. Thing
   c. Undefined
   d. Undefined

101. A _____ is a part of a line that is bounded by two end points, and contains every point on the line between its end points.
   a. Thing
   b. Line segment0
   c. Undefined
   d. Undefined

102. _____ is a relation in Euclidean geometry among the three sides of a right triangle.
   a. Pythagorean Theorem0
   b. Thing
   c. Undefined
   d. Undefined

103. In geometry, an _____ is a point at which a line segment or ray terminates.

a. Thing
b. Endpoint0
c. Undefined
d. Undefined

104. In mathematics, a _____ is a statement that can be proved on the basis of explicitly stated or previously agreed assumptions.
a. Thing
b. Theorem0
c. Undefined
d. Undefined

105. A _____ is one of the basic shapes of geometry: a polygon with three vertices and three sides which are straight line segments.
a. Triangle0
b. Thing
c. Undefined
d. Undefined

106. The _____ integers are all the integers from zero on upwards.
a. Thing
b. Nonnegative0
c. Undefined
d. Undefined

107. The _____ of measurement are a globally standardized and modernized form of the metric system.
a. Units0
b. Thing
c. Undefined
d. Undefined

108. Initial objects are also called _____, and terminal objects are also called final.
a. Thing
b. Coterminal0
c. Undefined
d. Undefined

109. _____ are a measure of time.
a. Thing
b. Minutes0
c. Undefined
d. Undefined

110. _____ is the middle point of a line segment.
a. Thing
b. Midpoint0
c. Undefined
d. Undefined

111. In mathematics, the concept of a _____ tries to capture the intuitive idea of a geometrical one-dimensional and continuous object. A simple example is the circle.
a. Thing
b. Curve0
c. Undefined
d. Undefined

112. In elementary algebra, an _____ is a set that contains every real number between two indicated numbers and may contain the two numbers themselves.
a. Interval0
b. Thing
c. Undefined
d. Undefined

113. The word _____ comes from the Latin word linearis, which means created by lines.

Chapter 1. Introduction To Functions and Graphs

    a. Linear0
    c. Undefined
    b. Thing
    d. Undefined

114. In geographic information systems, a _____ comprises an entity with a geographic location, typically determined by points, arcs, or polygons. Carriageways and cadastres exemplify _____ data.
    a. Thing
    c. Undefined
    b. Feature0
    d. Undefined

115. In geometry, a _____ is defined as a quadrilateral where all four of its angles are right angles.
    a. Rectangle0
    c. Undefined
    b. Thing
    d. Undefined

116. In mathematics, a set is called _____ if there is a bijection between the set and some set of the form {1, 2, ..., n} where n is a natural number.
    a. Finite0
    c. Undefined
    b. Thing
    d. Undefined

117. _____ are the basic objects of study in graph theory. Informally speaking, a graph is a set of objects called points, nodes, or vertices connected by links called lines or edges.
    a. Graphs0
    c. Undefined
    b. Thing
    d. Undefined

118. An _____ is when two lines intersect somewhere on a plane creating a right angle at intersection
    a. Thing
    c. Undefined
    b. Axes0
    d. Undefined

119. _____ means in succession or back-to-back
    a. Consecutive0
    c. Undefined
    b. Thing
    d. Undefined

120. The deductive-nomological model is a formalized view of scientific _____ in natural language.
    a. Thing
    c. Undefined
    b. Explanation0
    d. Undefined

121. _____ is a form of periodic payment from an employer to an employee, which is specified in an employment contract.
    a. Gross pay0
    c. Undefined
    b. Thing
    d. Undefined

122. A _____ is a form of periodic payment from an employer to an employee, which is specified in an employment contract.
    a. Salary0
    c. Undefined
    b. Thing
    d. Undefined

123. An _____ triange is a triangle with at least two sides of equal length.

a. Isosceles0   b. Thing
c. Undefined   d. Undefined

124. In geometry, a _____ is a special kind of point, usually a corner of a polygon, polyhedron, or higher dimensional polytope. In the geometry of curves a _____ is a point of where the first derivative of curvature is zero. In graph theory, a _____ is the fundamental unit out of which graphs are formed
   a. Thing   b. Vertex0
   c. Undefined   d. Undefined

125. In geometry, an _____ polygon is a polygon which has all sides of the same length.
   a. Thing   b. Equilateral0
   c. Undefined   d. Undefined

126. _____ is a statistical measure of the average length of survival of a living thing.
   a. Thing   b. Life expectancy0
   c. Undefined   d. Undefined

127. A _____ is a symbolic representation denoting a quantity or expression. It often represents an "unknown" quantity that has the potential to change.
   a. Variable0   b. Thing
   c. Undefined   d. Undefined

128. _____ is the level of functional and/or metabolic efficiency of an organism at both the micro level.
   a. Thing   b. Health0
   c. Undefined   d. Undefined

129. In mathematics, there are several meanings of _____ depending on the subject.
   a. Thing   b. Degree0
   c. Undefined   d. Undefined

130. The mathematical concept of a _____ expresses the intuitive idea of deterministic dependence between two quantities, one of which is viewed as primary and the other as secondary. A _____ then is a way to associate a unique output for each input of a specified type, for example, a real number or an element of a given set.
   a. Thing   b. Function0
   c. Undefined   d. Undefined

131. Mathematical _____ are the wide variety of ways to capture an abstract mathematical concept or relationship.
   a. Representations0   b. Thing
   c. Undefined   d. Undefined

132. _____ or arithmetics is the oldest and most elementary branch of mathematics, used by almost everyone, for tasks ranging from simple daily counting to advanced science and business calculations.
   a. Thing   b. Arithmetic0
   c. Undefined   d. Undefined

Chapter 1. Introduction To Functions and Graphs

133. In mathematics, an _____ is any of the arguments, i.e. "inputs", to a function. Thus if we have a function f(x), then x is a _____.
   a. Thing
   b. Independent variable0
   c. Undefined
   d. Undefined

134. In a function the _____, is the variable which is the value, i.e. the "output", of the function.
   a. Thing
   b. Dependent variable0
   c. Undefined
   d. Undefined

135. In statistics, a _____ measure is one which is measuring what is supposed to measure.
   a. Valid0
   b. Thing
   c. Undefined
   d. Undefined

136. The _____ is that number multiplied by itself.
   a. Thing
   b. Square of a number0
   c. Undefined
   d. Undefined

137. Leonhard _____ was a pioneering Swiss mathematician and physicist, who spent most of his life in Russia and Germany.
   a. Euler0
   b. Person
   c. Undefined
   d. Undefined

138. _____ was a pioneering Swiss mathematician and physicist, who spent most of his life in Russia and Germany.
   a. Leonhard Euler0
   b. Person
   c. Undefined
   d. Undefined

139. In mathematics, the _____ f is the collection of all ordered pairs . In particular, graph means the graphical representation of this collection, in the form of a curve or surface, together with axes, etc. Graphing on a Cartesian plane is sometimes referred to as curve sketching.
   a. Graph of a function0
   b. Thing
   c. Undefined
   d. Undefined

140. In mathematics, a _____ occurs if there is a bijection between the set and some set of the form 1, 2, ..., n where n is a natural number.
   a. Concept
   b. Finite set0
   c. Undefined
   d. Undefined

141. _____ is the state of being greater than any finite real or natural number, however large.
   a. Thing
   b. Infinite0
   c. Undefined
   d. Undefined

142. In set theory, an _____ is a set that is not a finite set. Infinite sets may be countable or uncountable.
   a. Infinite set0
   b. Thing
   c. Undefined
   d. Undefined

Chapter 1. Introduction To Functions and Graphs

143. In financial mathematics, the _____ volatility of an option contract is the volatility _____ by the market price of the option based on an option pricing model.
   a. Implied0
   b. Thing
   c. Undefined
   d. Undefined

144. In elementary algebra, a _____ is a polynomial with two terms: the sum of two monomials. It is the simplest kind of polynomial except for a monomial.
   a. Binomial0
   b. Thing
   c. Undefined
   d. Undefined

145. In geometry, an _____ of a triangle is a straight line through a vertex and perpendicular to (i.e. forming a right angle with) the opposite side or an extension of the opposite side.
   a. Altitude0
   b. Concept
   c. Undefined
   d. Undefined

146. A _____ fraction is a fraction in which the absolute value of the numerator is less than the denominator--hence, the absolute value of the fraction is less than 1.
   a. Proper0
   b. Thing
   c. Undefined
   d. Undefined

147. _____ the expected value of a random variable displays the average or central value of the variable. It is a summary value of the distribution of the variable.
   a. Determining0
   b. Thing
   c. Undefined
   d. Undefined

148. _____ is a test to determine if a relation or its graph is a function or not
   a. Thing
   b. Vertical line test0
   c. Undefined
   d. Undefined

149. A _____ is a simplified and structured visual representation of concepts, ideas, constructions, relations, statistical data, anatomy etc used in all aspects of human activities to visualize and clarify the topic.
   a. Diagram0
   b. Thing
   c. Undefined
   d. Undefined

150. A _____ is a statement or claimt that a particular event will occur in the future in more certain terms than a forecast.
   a. Thing
   b. Prediction0
   c. Undefined
   d. Undefined

151. _____ systems represent systems whose behavior is not expressible as a sum of the behaviors of its descriptors.
   a. Thing
   b. Nonlinear0
   c. Undefined
   d. Undefined

152. A _____ is a first degree polynomial mathematical function of the form: $f(x) = mx + b$ where m and b are real constants and x is a real variable.

Chapter 1. Introduction To Functions and Graphs 17

    a. Thing
    c. Undefined
    b. Linear function0
    d. Undefined

153. In mathematics and the mathematical sciences, a _____ is a fixed, but possibly unspecified, value. This is in contrast to a variable, which is not fixed.
    a. Thing
    c. Undefined
    b. Constant0
    d. Undefined

154. _____ is a function whose values do not vary and thus are constant.
    a. Thing
    c. Undefined
    b. Constant function0
    d. Undefined

155. A _____ function is a function for which, intuitively, small changes in the input result in small changes in the output.
    a. Continuous0
    c. Undefined
    b. Event
    d. Undefined

156. The word _____ comes from the 15th Century Latin word discretus which means separate.
    a. Thing
    c. Undefined
    b. Discrete0
    d. Undefined

157. A _____ is a function for which, intuitively, small changes in the input result in small changes in the output.
    a. Event
    c. Undefined
    b. Continuous function0
    d. Undefined

158. _____ is a state located in the southern and southwestern regions of the United States of America.
    a. Thing
    c. Undefined
    b. Texas0
    d. Undefined

159. In mathematics, defined and _____ are used to explain whether or not expressions have meaningful, sensible, and unambiguous values.
    a. Thing
    c. Undefined
    b. Undefined0
    d. Undefined

160. _____ of a curve is a line that intersects two or more points on the curve.
    a. Secant line0
    c. Undefined
    b. Thing
    d. Undefined

161. _____ is a trigonometric function that is the reciprocal of cosine.
    a. Secant0
    c. Undefined
    b. Thing
    d. Undefined

162. _____ of an object is its speed in a particular direction.
    a. Thing
    c. Undefined
    b. Velocity0
    d. Undefined

163. Regrouping is the act of putting ones into groups of 10. For example, the 1 on the far right of 131 would be denoted _____ if the digit of the number being subtracted is larger than 1, such as 131-99.
   a. By 100
   b. Thing
   c. Undefined
   d. Undefined

164. In mathematics, a _____ is the end result of a division problem. It can also be expressed as the number of times the divisor divides into the dividend.
   a. Quotient0
   b. Thing
   c. Undefined
   d. Undefined

165. _____ is a mathematical subject that includes the study of limits, derivatives, integrals, and power series and constitutes a major part of modern university curriculum.
   a. Calculus0
   b. Thing
   c. Undefined
   d. Undefined

166. The function difference divided by the point difference is known as the _____
   a. Difference quotient0
   b. Thing
   c. Undefined
   d. Undefined

167. In mathematics, the _____ of a coordinate system is the point where the axes of the system intersect.
   a. Thing
   b. Origin0
   c. Undefined
   d. Undefined

168. _____ or investing is a term with several closely-related meanings in business management, finance and economics, related to saving or deferring consumption.
   a. Thing
   b. Investment0
   c. Undefined
   d. Undefined

169. Graphing on a Cartesian plane is sometimes referred to as _____.
   a. Curve sketching0
   b. Thing
   c. Undefined
   d. Undefined

170. A _____ is a three-dimensional geometric shape formed by straight lines through a fixed point (vertex) to the points of a fixed curve (directrix)
   a. Concept
   b. Cone0
   c. Undefined
   d. Undefined

171. A _____ is a unit of length in the metric system, equal to one thousand metres, the current SI base unit of length
   a. Thing
   b. Kilometer0
   c. Undefined
   d. Undefined

172. _____ is a temperature scale named after the German physicist Daniel Gabriel _____ , who proposed it in 1724.
   a. Fahrenheit0
   b. Thing
   c. Undefined
   d. Undefined

Chapter 1. Introduction To Functions and Graphs

173. _____ are external two-dimensional outlines, with the appearance or configuration of some thing - in contrast to the matter or content or substance of which it is composed.
   a. Thing
   b. Shapes0
   c. Undefined
   d. Undefined

174. In mathematics, _____ are the intuitive idea of a geometrical one-dimensional and continuous object.
   a. Curves0
   b. Thing
   c. Undefined
   d. Undefined

175. In mathematics, the _____ is a conic section generated by the intersection of a right circular conical surface and a plane parallel to a generating straight line of that surface. It can also be defined as locus of points in a plane which are equidistant from a given point.
   a. Parabola0
   b. Thing
   c. Undefined
   d. Undefined

176. A _____ is used on railways, which, together with railroad switches , guide trains without the need for steering.
   a. Thing
   b. Railroad track0
   c. Undefined
   d. Undefined

177. In logic and mathematics, logical _____ is a logical relation that holds between a set T of formulas and a formula B when every model (or interpretation or valuation) of T is also a model of B.
   a. Concept
   b. Implication0
   c. Undefined
   d. Undefined

178. A _____ is a deliberate process for transforming one or more inputs into one or more results.
   a. Thing
   b. Calculation0
   c. Undefined
   d. Undefined

179. The _____ of a geographic location is its height above a fixed reference point, often the mean sea level.
   a. Elevation0
   b. Thing
   c. Undefined
   d. Undefined

180. _____ is the flow of blood in the cardiovascular system.
   a. Thing
   b. Blood flow0
   c. Undefined
   d. Undefined

Chapter 2. Linear Functions and Equations

1. An _____ is a combination of numbers, operators, grouping symbols and/or free variables and bound variables arranged in a meaningful way which can be evaluated..
   - a. Thing
   - b. Expression0
   - c. Undefined
   - d. Undefined

2. A _____ is a simplified and structured visual representation of concepts, ideas, constructions, relations, statistical data, anatomy etc used in all aspects of human activities to visualize and clarify the topic.
   - a. Thing
   - b. Diagram0
   - c. Undefined
   - d. Undefined

3. _____ is the scientific study of celestial objects such as stars, planets, comets, and galaxies; and phenomena that originate outside the Earth's atmosphere.
   - a. Thing
   - b. Astronomy0
   - c. Undefined
   - d. Undefined

4. _____, Greek for "knowledge of nature," is the branch of science concerned with the discovery and characterization of universal laws which govern matter, energy, space, and time.
   - a. Thing
   - b. Physics0
   - c. Undefined
   - d. Undefined

5. _____ is a synonym for information.
   - a. Data0
   - b. Thing
   - c. Undefined
   - d. Undefined

6. A _____ is a statement or claimt that a particular event will occur in the future in more certain terms than a forecast.
   - a. Thing
   - b. Prediction0
   - c. Undefined
   - d. Undefined

7. _____ are external two-dimensional outlines, with the appearance or configuration of some thing - in contrast to the matter or content or substance of which it is composed.
   - a. Thing
   - b. Shapes0
   - c. Undefined
   - d. Undefined

8. In epidemiology, an _____ is a disease that appears as new cases in a given human population, during a given period, at a rate that substantially exceeds with is "expected," based on recent experience.
   - a. Epidemic0
   - b. Thing
   - c. Undefined
   - d. Undefined

9. A _____ is an abstract model that uses mathematical language to describe the behavior of a system. Eykhoff defined a _____ as 'a representation of the essential aspects of an existing system which presents knowledge of that system in usable form'.
   - a. Thing
   - b. Mathematical model0
   - c. Undefined
   - d. Undefined

10. Multiple Signal Classification, also known as _____, is an algorithm used for frequency estimation and emitter location.

Chapter 2. Linear Functions and Equations

    a. Music0   b. Thing
    c. Undefined   d. Undefined

11. The word _____ comes from the Latin word linearis, which means created by lines.
    a. Linear0   b. Thing
    c. Undefined   d. Undefined

12. A _____ is a first degree polynomial mathematical function of the form: f(x) = mx + b where m and b are real constants and x is a real variable.
    a. Linear function0   b. Thing
    c. Undefined   d. Undefined

13. _____ is a kind of property which exists as magnitude or multitude. It is among the basic classes of things along with quality, substance, change, and relation.
    a. Thing   b. Amount0
    c. Undefined   d. Undefined

14. The mathematical concept of a _____ expresses the intuitive idea of deterministic dependence between two quantities, one of which is viewed as primary and the other as secondary. A _____ then is a way to associate a unique output for each input of a specified type, for example, a real number or an element of a given set.
    a. Thing   b. Function0
    c. Undefined   d. Undefined

15. Mathematical _____ are the wide variety of ways to capture an abstract mathematical concept or relationship.
    a. Thing   b. Representations0
    c. Undefined   d. Undefined

16. _____ are the basic objects of study in graph theory. Informally speaking, a graph is a set of objects called points, nodes, or vertices connected by links called lines or edges.
    a. Thing   b. Graphs0
    c. Undefined   d. Undefined

17. The _____ of measurement are a globally standardized and modernized form of the metric system.
    a. Units0   b. Thing
    c. Undefined   d. Undefined

18. _____ is often used to describe the measurement of the steepness, incline, gradient, or grade of a straight line. The _____ is defined as the ratio of the "rise" divided by the "run" between two points on a line, or in other words, the ratio of the altitude change to the horizontal distance between any two points on the line.
    a. Thing   b. Slope0
    c. Undefined   d. Undefined

19. A _____ is a special kind of ratio, indicating a relationship between two measurements with different units, such as miles to gallons or cents to pounds.

Chapter 2. Linear Functions and Equations

    a. Thing
    c. Undefined
    b. Rate0
    d. Undefined

20. In mathematics and the mathematical sciences, a _____ is a fixed, but possibly unspecified, value. This is in contrast to a variable, which is not fixed.
    a. Constant0
    c. Undefined
    b. Thing
    d. Undefined

21. Initial objects are also called _____, and terminal objects are also called final.
    a. Coterminal0
    c. Undefined
    b. Thing
    d. Undefined

22. U.S. liquid _____ is legally defined as 231 cubic inches, and is equal to 3.785411784 litres or abotu 0.13368 cubic feet. This is the most common definition of a _____. The U.S. fluid ounce is defined as 1/128 of a U.S. _____.
    a. Gallon0
    c. Undefined
    b. Thing
    d. Undefined

23. _____ are a measure of time.
    a. Thing
    c. Undefined
    b. Minutes0
    d. Undefined

24. A _____ is a symbolic representation denoting a quantity or expression. It often represents an "unknown" quantity that has the potential to change.
    a. Thing
    c. Undefined
    b. Variable0
    d. Undefined

25. In mathematics, a _____ of a k-place relation $L \subseteq X_1 \times \ldots \times X_k$ is one of the sets X_j, $1 \leq j \leq k$. In the special case where k = 2 and $L \subseteq X_1 \times X_2$ is a function $L : X_1 \to X_2$, it is conventional to refer to X_1 as the _____ of the function and to refer to X_2 as the codomain of the function.
    a. Thing
    c. Undefined
    b. Domain0
    d. Undefined

26. A _____ is a unit of length, usually used to measure distance, in a number of different systems, including Imperial units, United States customary units and Norwegian/Swedish mil. Its size can vary from system to system, but in each is between 1 and 10 kilometers. In contemporary English contexts _____ refers to either:
    a. Thing
    c. Undefined
    b. Mile0
    d. Undefined

27. _____ is a unit of speed, expressing the number of international miles covered per hour.
    a. Miles per hour0
    c. Undefined
    b. Thing
    d. Undefined

28. In mathematics, a _____ is any one of several different types of functions, mappings, operations, or transformations.

Chapter 2. Linear Functions and Equations

    a. Projection0   b. Thing
    c. Undefined   d. Undefined

29. In statistics, a _____ measure is one which is measuring what is supposed to measure.
    a. Thing   b. Valid0
    c. Undefined   d. Undefined

30. _____ means in succession or back-to-back
    a. Thing   b. Consecutive0
    c. Undefined   d. Undefined

31. A _____, scatter diagram or scatter graph is a graph used in statistics to visually display and relate two quantitative variables of a multidimensional data set by displaying the data as a collection of points, each having one coordinate on a horizontal and one on a vertical axis.
    a. Thing   b. Scatterplot0
    c. Undefined   d. Undefined

32. In geometry, a _____ is defined as a quadrilateral where all four of its angles are right angles.
    a. Rectangle0   b. Thing
    c. Undefined   d. Undefined

33. _____ is a regression method that models the relationship between a dependent variable Y, independent variables Xp, and a random term å.
    a. Thing   b. Linear regression0
    c. Undefined   d. Undefined

34. In probability theory and statistics, _____, also called _____ coefficient, indicates the strength and direction of a linear relationship between two random variables.
    a. Correlation0   b. Thing
    c. Undefined   d. Undefined

35. In mathematics, a _____ may be described informally as a number that can be given by an infinite decimal representation.
    a. Real number0   b. Thing
    c. Undefined   d. Undefined

36. In mathematics, a _____ is a constant multiplicative factor of a certain object. The object can be such things as a variable, a vector, a function, etc. For example, the _____ of $9x^2$ is 9.
    a. Thing   b. Coefficient0
    c. Undefined   d. Undefined

37. _____ the expected value of a random variable displays the average or central value of the variable. It is a summary value of the distribution of the variable.
    a. Thing   b. Determining0
    c. Undefined   d. Undefined

38. In mathematics, an _____, mean, or central tendency of a data set refers to a measure of the "middle" or "expected" value of the data set.
   a. Concept
   b. Average0
   c. Undefined
   d. Undefined

39. _____, usually denoted symbolically by the Greek letter phi, Î¦, gives the location of a place on Earth north or south of the equator. _____ is an angular measurement in degrees (marked with Â°) ranging from 0Â° at the Equator (low _____) to 90Â° at the poles (90Â° N for the North Pole or 90Â° S for the South Pole; high _____). The complementary angle of a _____ is called the colatitude.
   a. Latitude0
   b. Thing
   c. Undefined
   d. Undefined

40. _____ is a physical property of a system that underlies the common notions of hot and cold; something that is hotter has the greater _____.
   a. Temperature0
   b. Thing
   c. Undefined
   d. Undefined

41. In geographic information systems, a _____ comprises an entity with a geographic location, typically determined by points, arcs, or polygons. Carriageways and cadastres exemplify _____ data.
   a. Thing
   b. Feature0
   c. Undefined
   d. Undefined

42. In mathematics, the _____ of a coordinate system is the point where the axes of the system intersect.
   a. Origin0
   b. Thing
   c. Undefined
   d. Undefined

43. In classical geometry, a _____ of a circle or sphere is any line segment from its center to its boundary. By extension, the _____ of a circle or sphere is the length of any such segment. The _____ is half the diameter. In science and engineering the term _____ of curvature is commonly used as a synonym for _____.
   a. Radius0
   b. Thing
   c. Undefined
   d. Undefined

44. In Euclidean geometry, a _____ is the set of all points in a plane at a fixed distance, called the radius, from a given point, the center.
   a. Circle0
   b. Thing
   c. Undefined
   d. Undefined

45. _____ of an object is its speed in a particular direction.
   a. Velocity0
   b. Thing
   c. Undefined
   d. Undefined

46. Transport or _____ is the movement of people and goods from one place to another.
   a. Transportation0
   b. Thing
   c. Undefined
   d. Undefined

Chapter 2. Linear Functions and Equations

47. In mathematics, a _____ is a mathematical statement which appears likely to be true, but has not been formally proven to be true under the rules of mathematical logic.
- a. Conjecture0
- b. Concept
- c. Undefined
- d. Undefined

48. A _____ is a deliberate process for transforming one or more inputs into one or more results.
- a. Calculation0
- b. Thing
- c. Undefined
- d. Undefined

49. The _____ is defined as the summation of all particles and energy that exist and the space-time which all events occur.
- a. Thing
- b. Universe0
- c. Undefined
- d. Undefined

50. The _____ of a solid object is the three-dimensional concept of how much space it occupies, often quantified numerically.
- a. Thing
- b. Volume0
- c. Undefined
- d. Undefined

51. In mathematics, the concept of a _____ tries to capture the intuitive idea of a geometrical one-dimensional and continuous object. A simple example is the circle.
- a. Curve0
- b. Thing
- c. Undefined
- d. Undefined

52. In mathematics, _____ is the process of constructing new data points outside a discrete set of known data points. It is similar to the process of interpolation, which constructs new points between known points, but its results are often less meaningful, and are subject to greater uncertainty.
- a. Extrapolation0
- b. Thing
- c. Undefined
- d. Undefined

53. In astronomy, geography, geometry and related sciences and contexts, a plane is said to be _____ at a given point if it is locally perpendicular to the gradient of the gravity field, i.e., with the direction of the gravitational force at that point.
- a. Horizontal0
- b. Thing
- c. Undefined
- d. Undefined

54. Any point where a graph makes contact with an coordinate axis is called an _____ of the graph
- a. Intercept0
- b. Thing
- c. Undefined
- d. Undefined

55. In geometry, two lines or planes if one falls on the other in such a way as to create congruent adjacent angles. The term may be used as a noun or adjective. Thus, referring to Figure 1, the line AB is the _____ to CD through the point B.
- a. Perpendicular0
- b. Thing
- c. Undefined
- d. Undefined

56. _____ is a method of constructing new data points from a discrete set of known data points.

a. Interpolation0
b. Thing
c. Undefined
d. Undefined

57. In mathematics and logic, a _____ proof is a way of showing the truth or falsehood of a given statement by a straightforward combination of established facts, usually existing lemmas and theorems, without making any further assumptions.
   a. Direct0
   b. Thing
   c. Undefined
   d. Undefined

58. _____ is the relationship between two variables, like a ratio in which the two quantities being compared are different units.
   a. Thing
   b. Direct variation0
   c. Undefined
   d. Undefined

59. Equivalence is the condition of being _____ or essentially equal.
   a. Equivalent0
   b. Thing
   c. Undefined
   d. Undefined

60. _____ is a branch of mathematics concerning the study of structure, relation and quantity.
   a. Algebra0
   b. Concept
   c. Undefined
   d. Undefined

61. In mathematics, and in particular in abstract algebra, the _____ is a property of binary operations that generalises the distributive law from elementary algebra.
   a. Distributive property0
   b. Thing
   c. Undefined
   d. Undefined

62. _____ or investing is a term with several closely-related meanings in business management, finance and economics, related to saving or deferring consumption.
   a. Investment0
   b. Thing
   c. Undefined
   d. Undefined

63. In mathematics, a _____ or rhodonea curve is a sinusoid plotted in polar coordinates.
   a. Rose0
   b. Thing
   c. Undefined
   d. Undefined

64. In geometry, a line _____ is a part of a line that is bounded by two end points, and contains every point on the line between its end points.
   a. Concept
   b. Segment0
   c. Undefined
   d. Undefined

65. A _____ is a part of a line that is bounded by two end points, and contains every point on the line between its end points.
   a. Thing
   b. Line segment0
   c. Undefined
   d. Undefined

Chapter 2. Linear Functions and Equations

66. _____ is a notation for writing numbers that is often used by scientists and mathematicians to make it easier to write large and small numbers.
   a. Scientific notation0
   b. Thing
   c. Undefined
   d. Undefined

67. _____ is a function whose values do not vary and thus are constant.
   a. Thing
   b. Constant function0
   c. Undefined
   d. Undefined

68. The existence and properties of _____ are the basis of Euclid's parallel postulate. _____ are two lines on the same plane that do not intersect even assuming that lines extend to infinity in either direction.
   a. Parallel lines0
   b. Thing
   c. Undefined
   d. Undefined

69. In mathematics, a _____ is the result of multiplying, or an expression that identifies factors to be multiplied.
   a. Thing
   b. Product0
   c. Undefined
   d. Undefined

70. In mathematics, the multiplicative inverse of a number x, denoted 1/x or x^{-1}, is the number which, when multiplied by x, yields 1. The multiplicative inverse of x is also called the _____ of x.
   a. Reciprocal0
   b. Thing
   c. Undefined
   d. Undefined

71. The act of _____ is the calculated approximation of a result which is usable even if input data may be incomplete, uncertain, or noisy.
   a. Estimating0
   b. Thing
   c. Undefined
   d. Undefined

72. In mathematics, two quantities are called _____ if they vary in such a way that one of the quantities is a constant multiple of the other, or equivalently if they have a constant ratio.
   a. Thing
   b. Proportional0
   c. Undefined
   d. Undefined

73. In mathematics, a _____ is an n-tuple with n being 3.
   a. Thing
   b. Triple0
   c. Undefined
   d. Undefined

74. _____ is a special mathematical relationship between two quantities. Two quantities are called proportional if they vary in such a way that one of the quantities is a constant multiple of the other, or equivalently if they have a constant ratio.
   a. Proportionality0
   b. Thing
   c. Undefined
   d. Undefined

75. An _____ is a collection of two not necessarily distinct objects, one of which is distinguished as the first coordinate and the other as the second coordinate.

Chapter 2. Linear Functions and Equations

    a. Thing
    c. Undefined
    b. Ordered pair0
    d. Undefined

76. In mathematics, the conjugate _____ or adjoint matrix of an m-by-n matrix A with complex entries is the n-by-m matrix A* obtained from A by taking the transpose and then taking the complex conjugate of each entry.
    a. Pairs0
    c. Undefined
    b. Thing
    d. Undefined

77. A _____ is a quantity that denotes the proportional amount or magnitude of one quantity relative to another.
    a. Thing
    c. Undefined
    b. Ratio0
    d. Undefined

78. In mathematics, a subset of Euclidean space R^n is called _____ if it is closed and bounded.
    a. Compact0
    c. Undefined
    b. Thing
    d. Undefined

79. A _____ is a consumption tax charged at the point of purchase for certain goods and services.
    a. Sales tax0
    c. Undefined
    b. Thing
    d. Undefined

80. In a mathematical proof or a syllogism, a _____ is a statement that is the logical consequence of preceding statements.
    a. Conclusion0
    c. Undefined
    b. Concept
    d. Undefined

81. In mathematics and more specifically set theory, the _____ set is the unique set which contains no elements.
    a. Thing
    c. Undefined
    b. Empty0
    d. Undefined

82. A _____ is a compensation which workers receive in exchange for their labor.
    a. Thing
    c. Undefined
    b. Wage0
    d. Undefined

83. In sociology and biology a _____ is the collection of people or organisms of a particular species living in a given geographic area or space, usually measured by a census.
    a. Population0
    c. Undefined
    b. Thing
    d. Undefined

84. _____, in law and economics, is a form of risk management primarily used to hedge against the risk of a contingent loss.
    a. Insurance0
    c. Undefined
    b. Thing
    d. Undefined

85. In geometry, the _____ of an object is a point in some sense in the middle of the object.

a. Thing
b. Center0
c. Undefined
d. Undefined

86. Acid _____ ratio measures the ability of a company to use its near cash or quick assets to immediately extinguish its current liabilities.
a. Test0
b. Thing
c. Undefined
d. Undefined

87. In plane geometry, a _____ is a polygon with four equal sides, four right angles, and parallel opposite sides. In algebra, the _____ of a number is that number multiplied by itself.
a. Thing
b. Square0
c. Undefined
d. Undefined

88. _____ is electromagnetic radiation with a wavelength that is visible to the eye (visible _____) or, in a technical or scientific context, electromagnetic radiation of any wavelength.
a. Thing
b. Light0
c. Undefined
d. Undefined

89. In geometry, an _____ of a triangle is a straight line through a vertex and perpendicular to (i.e. forming a right angle with) the opposite side or an extension of the opposite side.
a. Altitude0
b. Concept
c. Undefined
d. Undefined

90. In Euclidean geometry, a uniform _____ is a linear transformation that enlargers or diminishes objects, and whose _____ factor is the same in all directions. This is also called homothethy.
a. Scale0
b. Thing
c. Undefined
d. Undefined

91. In physics, _____ is an influence that may cause an object to accelerate. It may be experienced as a lift, a push, or a pull. The actual acceleration of the body is determined by the vector sum of all forces acting on it, known as net _____ or resultant _____.
a. Thing
b. Force0
c. Undefined
d. Undefined

92. In business, particularly accounting, a _____ is the time intervals that the accounts, statement, payments, or other calculations cover.
a. Thing
b. Period0
c. Undefined
d. Undefined

93. _____ is a subset of a population.
a. Thing
b. Sample0
c. Undefined
d. Undefined

94. A _____ is an equation in which each term is either a constant or the product of a constant times the first power of a variable.

Chapter 2. Linear Functions and Equations

a. Linear equation0
b. Thing
c. Undefined
d. Undefined

95. In mathematics, the word _____ is used informally to refer to certain distinct bodies of knowledge about mathematics.
 a. Thing
 b. Theoretical0
 c. Undefined
 d. Undefined

96. In the context of spaceflight, a _____ are any object which has been placed into orbit by human endeavor.
 a. Thing
 b. Satellites0
 c. Undefined
 d. Undefined

97. _____, are a medical imaging method employing tomography where digital geometry processing is used to generate a three-dimensional image of the internals of an object from a large series of two-dimensional X-ray images taken around a single axis of rotation.
 a. CAT scans0
 b. Thing
 c. Undefined
 d. Undefined

98. In common philosophical language, a proposition or _____, is the content of an assertion, that is, it is true-or-false and defined by the meaning of a particular piece of language.
 a. Statement0
 b. Concept
 c. Undefined
 d. Undefined

99. The _____, the average in everyday English, which is also called the arithmetic _____ (and is distinguished from the geometric _____ or harmonic _____). The average is also called the sample _____. The expected value of a random variable, which is also called the population _____.
 a. Thing
 b. Mean0
 c. Undefined
 d. Undefined

100. A _____ is a set of possible values that a variable can take on in order to satisfy a given set of conditions, which may include equations and inequalities.
 a. Thing
 b. Solution set0
 c. Undefined
 d. Undefined

101. An _____ is an equality that remains true regardless of the values of any variables that appear within it, to distinguish it from an equality which is true under more particular conditions.
 a. Identity0
 b. Thing
 c. Undefined
 d. Undefined

102. The material _____, also known as the material implication or truth functional _____, expresses a property of certain conditionals in logic.
 a. Conditional0
 b. Thing
 c. Undefined
 d. Undefined

103. _____ systems represent systems whose behavior is not expressible as a sum of the behaviors of its descriptors.

Chapter 2. Linear Functions and Equations

  a. Thing   b. Nonlinear0
  c. Undefined   d. Undefined

104. Two mathematical objects are equal if and only if they are precisely the same in every way. This defines a binary relation, _____, denoted by the sign of _____ "=" in such a way that the statement "x = y" means that x and y are equal.
  a. Thing   b. Equality0
  c. Undefined   d. Undefined

105. In mathematics, _____ is an elementary arithmetic operation. When one of the numbers is a whole number, _____ is the repeated sum of the other number.
  a. Multiplication0   b. Thing
  c. Undefined   d. Undefined

106. A _____ is a negotiable instrument instructing a financial institution to pay a specific amount of a specific currency from a specific demand account held in the maker/depositor's name with that institution. Both the maker and payee may be natural persons or legal entities.
  a. Check0   b. Thing
  c. Undefined   d. Undefined

107. A _____ is the part of a fraction that tells how many equal parts make up a whole, and which is used in the name of the fraction: "halves", "thirds", "fourths" or "quarters", "fifths" and so on.
  a. Concept   b. Denominator0
  c. Undefined   d. Undefined

108. In mathematics, the _____ of two sets A and B is the set that contains all elements of A that also belong to B (or equivalently, all elements of B that also belong to A), but no other elements.
  a. Thing   b. Intersection0
  c. Undefined   d. Undefined

109. _____ is a way of expressing a number as a fraction of 100 per cent meaning "per hundred".
  a. Thing   b. Percent0
  c. Undefined   d. Undefined

110. A _____ function is a function for which, intuitively, small changes in the input result in small changes in the output.
  a. Event   b. Continuous0
  c. Undefined   d. Undefined

111. In elementary algebra, an _____ is a set that contains every real number between two indicated numbers and may contain the two numbers themselves.
  a. Interval0   b. Thing
  c. Undefined   d. Undefined

112. In mathematics, _____ are essentially word problems that are designed to use mathematical critical thinking in everyday situations.

a. Application problems0
b. Thing
c. Undefined
d. Undefined

113. _____ is the transport of people on a trip/journey or the process or time involved in a person or object moving from one location to another.
   a. Travel0
   b. Thing
   c. Undefined
   d. Undefined

114. A _____ is one of the basic shapes of geometry: a polygon with three vertices and three sides which are straight line segments.
   a. Thing
   b. Triangle0
   c. Undefined
   d. Undefined

115. A _____, lamp post, street lamp, light standard or lamp standard, is a raised source of light on the edge of a road, turned on or lit at a certain time every night.
   a. Streetlight0
   b. Thing
   c. Undefined
   d. Undefined

116. In probability theory and statistics, a _____ is a number dividing the higher half of a sample, a population, or a probability distribution from the lower half.
   a. Concept
   b. Median0
   c. Undefined
   d. Undefined

117. The _____ (symbol _____) and the millibar (symbol mbar, also mb) are units of pressure.
   a. Thing
   b. Bar0
   c. Undefined
   d. Undefined

118. In physics, an _____ is the path that an object makes around another object while under the influence of a source of centripetal force, such as gravity.
   a. Orbit0
   b. Thing
   c. Undefined
   d. Undefined

119. _____ is mass m per unit volume V.
   a. Thing
   b. Density0
   c. Undefined
   d. Undefined

120. A _____ is a three-dimensional geometric shape formed by straight lines through a fixed point (vertex) to the points of a fixed curve (directrix)
   a. Concept
   b. Cone0
   c. Undefined
   d. Undefined

121. In geometry, a _____ (Greek words diairo = divide and metro = measure) of a circle is any straight line segment that passes through the centre and whose endpoints are on the circular boundary, or, in more modern usage, the length of such a line segment. When using the word in the more modern sense, one speaks of the _____ rather than a _____, because all diameters of a circle have the same length. This length is twice the radius. The _____ of a circle is also the longest chord that the circle has.

Chapter 2. Linear Functions and Equations

    a. Thing
    b. Diameter0
    c. Undefined
    d. Undefined

122. In mathematics, a _____ function in the sense of algebraic geometry is an everywhere-defined, polynomial function on an algebraic variety V with values in the field K over which V is defined.
    a. Regular0
    b. Thing
    c. Undefined
    d. Undefined

123. _____ is the distance around a given two-dimensional object. As a general rule, the _____ of a polygon can always be calculated by adding all the length of the sides together. So, the formula for triangles is P = a + b + c, where a, b and c stand for each side of it. For quadrilaterals the equation is P = a + b + c + d. For equilateral polygons, P = na, where n is the number of sides and a is the side length.
    a. Perimeter0
    b. Thing
    c. Undefined
    d. Undefined

124. In chemistry, a _____ is substance made by combining two or more different materials in such a way that no chemical reaction occurs.
    a. Mixture0
    b. Thing
    c. Undefined
    d. Undefined

125. _____ is the fee paid on borrowed money.
    a. Thing
    b. Interest0
    c. Undefined
    d. Undefined

126. _____ is a temperature scale named after the German physicist Daniel Gabriel _____ , who proposed it in 1724.
    a. Fahrenheit0
    b. Thing
    c. Undefined
    d. Undefined

127. The _____ is a temperature scale named after the German physicist Daniel Gabriel Fahrenheit (1686–1736), who proposed it in 1724.
    a. Thing
    b. Fahrenheit scale0
    c. Undefined
    d. Undefined

128. _____ is, or relates to, the _____ temperature scale .
    a. Thing
    b. Celsius0
    c. Undefined
    d. Undefined

129. A _____ given two distinct points A and B on the _____, is the set of points C on the line containing points A and B such that A is not strictly between C and B.
    a. Ray0
    b. Thing
    c. Undefined
    d. Undefined

130. In mathematics, the _____ f is the collection of all ordered pairs . In particular, graph means the graphical representation of this collection, in the form of a curve or surface, together with axes, etc. Graphing on a Cartesian plane is sometimes referred to as curve sketching.

Chapter 2. Linear Functions and Equations

a. Thing
c. Undefined
b. Graph of a function0
d. Undefined

131. In mathematics, an _____ is a statement about the relative size or order of two objects.
a. Inequality0
c. Undefined
b. Thing
d. Undefined

132. In mathematics, the _____ of a function is the set of all "output" values produced by that function. Given a function $f: A \to B$, the _____ of f, is defined to be the set $\{x \in B : x = f(a)$ for some $a \in A\}$.
a. Thing
c. Undefined
b. Range0
d. Undefined

133. An _____ is a term used to describe an allocation of money from one person to another.
a. Thing
c. Undefined
b. Allowance0
d. Undefined

134. Mathematical _____ is used to represent ideas.
a. Notation0
c. Undefined
b. Thing
d. Undefined

135. A _____ is a one-dimensional picture in which the integers are shown as specially-marked points evenly spaced on a line.
a. Number line0
c. Undefined
b. Thing
d. Undefined

136. _____ is the notation in which permitted values for a variable are expressed as ranging over a certain interval; "5 < x < 9" is an example of the application of _____.
a. Thing
c. Undefined
b. Interval notation0
d. Undefined

137. In geometry, an _____ is a point at which a line segment or ray terminates.
a. Thing
c. Undefined
b. Endpoint0
d. Undefined

138. _____, either of the curved-bracket punctuation marks that together make a set of _____
a. Thing
c. Undefined
b. Parentheses0
d. Undefined

139. _____ is the state of being greater than any finite number, however large.
a. Infinity0
c. Undefined
b. Thing
d. Undefined

140. In mathematics, an inequality is a statement about the relative size or order of two objects. For example 14 > 10, or 14 is _____ 10.

Chapter 2. Linear Functions and Equations

    a. Thing
    b. Greater than0
    c. Undefined
    d. Undefined

141. _____, from Latin meaning "to make progress", is defined in two different ways. Pure economic _____ is the increase in wealth that an investor has from making an investment, taking into consideration all costs associated with that investment including the opportunity cost of capital.
    a. Thing
    b. Profit0
    c. Undefined
    d. Undefined

142. _____ interest refers to the fact that whenever interest is calculated, it is based not only on the original principal, but also on any unpaid interest that has been added to the principal.
    a. Compound0
    b. Thing
    c. Undefined
    d. Undefined

143. The deductive-nomological model is a formalized view of scientific _____ in natural language.
    a. Thing
    b. Explanation0
    c. Undefined
    d. Undefined

144. A _____ is a type of debt. All material things can be lent but this article focuses exclusively on monetary loans. Like all debt instruments, a _____ entails the redistribution of financial assets over time, between the lender and the borrower.
    a. Loan0
    b. Thing
    c. Undefined
    d. Undefined

145. An _____ is the fee paid on borrow money.
    a. Interest rate0
    b. Concept
    c. Undefined
    d. Undefined

146. In mathematics a _____ is a function which defines a distance between elements of a set.
    a. Thing
    b. Metric0
    c. Undefined
    d. Undefined

147. _____ or arithmetics is the oldest and most elementary branch of mathematics, used by almost everyone, for tasks ranging from simple daily counting to advanced science and business calculations.
    a. Arithmetic0
    b. Thing
    c. Undefined
    d. Undefined

148. _____ of a list of numbers is the sum of all the members of the list divided by the number of items in the list.
    a. Thing
    b. Arithmetic mean0
    c. Undefined
    d. Undefined

149. A _____ defined function $f(x)$ of a real variable x is a function whose definition is given differently on disjoint subsets of its domain.
    a. Thing
    b. Piecewise0
    c. Undefined
    d. Undefined

Chapter 2. Linear Functions and Equations

150. In mathematics, the _____ (or modulus) of a real number is its numerical value without regard to its sign.
   a. Thing
   b. Absolute value0
   c. Undefined
   d. Undefined

151. A function on the real numbers is called a _____ if it can be written as a finite linear combination of indicator functions of half-open intervals.
   a. Step function0
   b. Thing
   c. Undefined
   d. Undefined

152. A _____ of a number is the product of that number with any integer.
   a. Multiple0
   b. Thing
   c. Undefined
   d. Undefined

153. In statistics, _____ means the most frequent value assumed by a random variable, or occurring in a sampling of a random variable.
   a. Concept
   b. Mode0
   c. Undefined
   d. Undefined

154. In mathematics, a _____ (also spelled reflexion) is a map that transforms an object into its mirror image.
   a. Reflection0
   b. Concept
   c. Undefined
   d. Undefined

155. In set theory and other branches of mathematics, the _____ of a collection of sets is the set that contains everything that belongs to any of the sets, but nothing else.
   a. Thing
   b. Union0
   c. Undefined
   d. Undefined

156. An _____ or member of a set is an object that when collected together make up the set.
   a. Thing
   b. Element0
   c. Undefined
   d. Undefined

157. In mathematics, the _____ , or members of a set or more generally a class are all those objects which when collected together make up the set or class.
   a. Thing
   b. Elements0
   c. Undefined
   d. Undefined

158. In mathematics, there are several meanings of _____ depending on the subject.
   a. Thing
   b. Degree0
   c. Undefined
   d. Undefined

159. _____ is the capital of the U.S. state of New Mexico.
   a. Santa Fe0
   b. Thing
   c. Undefined
   d. Undefined

160. _____, in economics and political economy, are the distributions or payments awarded to the various suppliers of the factors of production.

Chapter 2. Linear Functions and Equations

a. Returns0
b. Thing
c. Undefined
d. Undefined

161. The _____ is the distance around a closed curve. _____ is a kind of perimeter.
    a. Circumference0
    b. Thing
    c. Undefined
    d. Undefined

162. _____ is the estimation of a physical quantity such as distance, energy, temperature, or time.
    a. Measurement0
    b. Thing
    c. Undefined
    d. Undefined

163. In regression analysis, _____, also known as ordinary _____ analysis is a method for linear regression that determines the values of unknown quantities in a statistical model by minimizing the sum of the residuals difference between the predicted and observed values squared.
    a. Least squares0
    b. Thing
    c. Undefined
    d. Undefined

164. A _____ is a function that assigns a number to subsets of a given set.
    a. Thing
    b. Measure0
    c. Undefined
    d. Undefined

165. In mathematics, a matrix can be thought of as each row or _____ being a vector. Hence, a space formed by row vectors or _____ vectors are said to be a row space or a _____ space.
    a. Concept
    b. Column0
    c. Undefined
    d. Undefined

166. In mathematics, the additive inverse, or _____ of a number n is the number that, when added to n, yields zero. The additive inverse of n is denoted −n. For example, 7 is −7, because 7 + (−7) = 0, and the additive inverse of −0.3 is 0.3, because −0.3 + 0.3 = 0.
    a. Thing
    b. Opposite0
    c. Undefined
    d. Undefined

167. In mathematics, the _____ of a number n is the number that, when added to n, yields zero. The _____ of n is denoted −n. For example, 7 is −7, because 7 + (−7) = 0, and the _____ of −0.3 is 0.3, because −0.3 + 0.3 = 0.
    a. Additive inverse0
    b. Thing
    c. Undefined
    d. Undefined

168. A _____ is the result of the addition of a set of numbers. The numbers may be natural numbers, complex numbers, matrices, or still more complicated objects. An infinite _____ is a subtle procedure known as a series.
    a. Sum0
    b. Thing
    c. Undefined
    d. Undefined

169. A _____ is a unit of length in the metric system, equal to one thousand metres, the current SI base unit of length
    a. Thing
    b. Kilometer0
    c. Undefined
    d. Undefined

Chapter 2. Linear Functions and Equations

170. _____ is an adjective usually refering to being in the centre.
   a. Central0
   b. Thing
   c. Undefined
   d. Undefined

171. _____ is the level of functional and/or metabolic efficiency of an organism at both the micro level.
   a. Thing
   b. Health0
   c. Undefined
   d. Undefined

172. In linear algebra, the _____ of an n-by-n square matrix A is defined to be the sum of the elements on the main diagonal of A,
   a. Trace0
   b. Thing
   c. Undefined
   d. Undefined

173. In mathematics, a _____ is the end result of a division problem. It can also be expressed as the number of times the divisor divides into the dividend.
   a. Thing
   b. Quotient0
   c. Undefined
   d. Undefined

174. The function difference divided by the point difference is known as the _____
   a. Thing
   b. Difference quotient0
   c. Undefined
   d. Undefined

175. In mathematics, a _____ is a quadric surface, with the following equation in Cartesian coordinates: $(x/_a)^2 + (y/_b)^2 = 1$.
   a. Thing
   b. Cylinder0
   c. Undefined
   d. Undefined

176. _____ are any documents that aim to streamline particular processes according to a set routine.
   a. Thing
   b. Guidelines0
   c. Undefined
   d. Undefined

177. In the mathematical field of numerical analysis, the _____ in some data is the discrepancy between an exact value and some approximation to it.
   a. Thing
   b. Approximation Error0
   c. Undefined
   d. Undefined

178. A _____ is a polynomial function of the form $f(x) = ax^2 + bx + c$, where a, b, c are real numbers and a , 0.
   a. Event
   b. Quadratic function0
   c. Undefined
   d. Undefined

179. _____ are activities that are governed by a set of rules or customs and often engaged in competitively.
   a. Thing
   b. Sports0
   c. Undefined
   d. Undefined

180. In Euclidean geometry, an _____ is a closed segment of a differentiable curve in the two-dimensional plane; for example, a circular _____ is a segment of a circle.

a. Arc0
b. Concept
c. Undefined
d. Undefined

Chapter 3. Quadratic Functions and Equations

1. A _____ is a polynomial function of the form $f(x) = ax^2 + bx + c$, where a, b, c are real numbers and a , 0.
   a. Quadratic function0
   b. Event
   c. Undefined
   d. Undefined

2. _____ is a synonym for information.
   a. Thing
   b. Data0
   c. Undefined
   d. Undefined

3. The word _____ comes from the Latin word linearis, which means created by lines.
   a. Thing
   b. Linear0
   c. Undefined
   d. Undefined

4. A _____ is a first degree polynomial mathematical function of the form: $f(x) = mx + b$ where m and b are real constants and x is a real variable.
   a. Linear function0
   b. Thing
   c. Undefined
   d. Undefined

5. The mathematical concept of a _____ expresses the intuitive idea of deterministic dependence between two quantities, one of which is viewed as primary and the other as secondary. A _____ then is a way to associate a unique output for each input of a specified type, for example, a real number or an element of a given set.
   a. Function0
   b. Thing
   c. Undefined
   d. Undefined

6. _____ systems represent systems whose behavior is not expressible as a sum of the behaviors of its descriptors.
   a. Thing
   b. Nonlinear0
   c. Undefined
   d. Undefined

7. In mathematics, a _____ may be described informally as a number that can be given by an infinite decimal representation.
   a. Real number0
   b. Thing
   c. Undefined
   d. Undefined

8. In mathematics, a _____ of a k-place relation $L \subseteq X_1 \times ... \times X_k$ is one of the sets X_j, $1 \leq j \leq k$. In the special case where k = 2 and $L \subseteq X_1 \times X_2$ is a function $L : X_1 \to X_2$, it is conventional to refer to X_1 as the _____ of the function and to refer to X_2 as the codomain of the function.
   a. Domain0
   b. Thing
   c. Undefined
   d. Undefined

9. In mathematics, a _____ is a constant multiplicative factor of a certain object. The object can be such things as a variable, a vector, a function, etc. For example, the _____ of $9x^2$ is 9.
   a. Thing
   b. Coefficient0
   c. Undefined
   d. Undefined

10. _____ are the basic objects of study in graph theory. Informally speaking, a graph is a set of objects called points, nodes, or vertices connected by links called lines or edges.

Chapter 3. Quadratic Functions and Equations

a. Graphs0
b. Thing
c. Undefined
d. Undefined

11. In mathematics, the _____ is a conic section generated by the intersection of a right circular conical surface and a plane parallel to a generating straight line of that surface. It can also be defined as locus of points in a plane which are equidistant from a given point.
    a. Thing
    b. Parabola0
    c. Undefined
    d. Undefined

12. In geometry, a _____ is a special kind of point, usually a corner of a polygon, polyhedron, or higher dimensional polytope. In the geometry of curves a _____ is a point of where the first derivative of curvature is zero. In graph theory, a _____ is the fundamental unit out of which graphs are formed
    a. Thing
    b. Vertex0
    c. Undefined
    d. Undefined

13. In plane geometry, a _____ is a polygon with four equal sides, four right angles, and parallel opposite sides. In algebra, the _____ of a number is that number multiplied by itself.
    a. Square0
    b. Thing
    c. Undefined
    d. Undefined

14. _____ means "constancy", i.e. if something retains a certain feature even after we change a way of looking at it, then it is symmetric.
    a. Thing
    b. Symmetry0
    c. Undefined
    d. Undefined

15. An _____ is a straight line around which a geometric figure can be rotated.
    a. Axis0
    b. Thing
    c. Undefined
    d. Undefined

16. _____ of a two-dimensional figure is a line such that, if a perpendicular is constructed, any two points lying on the perpendicular at equal distances from the _____ are identical.
    a. Axis of symmetry0
    b. Thing
    c. Undefined
    d. Undefined

17. A _____ is a set of numbers that designate location in a given reference system, such as x,y in a planar _____ system or an x,y,z in a three-dimensional _____ system.
    a. Thing
    b. Coordinate0
    c. Undefined
    d. Undefined

18. _____ is a technique used in algebra to solve quadratic equations, in analytic geometry for determining the shapes of graphs, and in calculus for computing integrals, including, but hardly limited to, the integrals that define Laplace transforms. The essential objective is to reduce a quadratic polynomial in a variable in an equation or expression to a squared polynomial of linear order. This can reduce an equation or integral to one that is more easily solved or evaluated.
    a. Completing the square0
    b. Thing
    c. Undefined
    d. Undefined

Chapter 3. Quadratic Functions and Equations

19. An _____ is a combination of numbers, operators, grouping symbols and/or free variables and bound variables arranged in a meaningful way which can be evaluated..
    a. Thing
    b. Expression0
    c. Undefined
    d. Undefined

20. _____ is a branch of mathematics concerning the study of structure, relation and quantity.
    a. Concept
    b. Algebra0
    c. Undefined
    d. Undefined

21. In elementary algebra, a _____ is a polynomial with two terms: the sum of two monomials. It is the simplest kind of polynomial except for a monomial.
    a. Thing
    b. Binomial0
    c. Undefined
    d. Undefined

22. A _____ is a polynomial consisting of three terms; in other words, it is the sum of three monomials.
    a. Trinomial0
    b. Thing
    c. Undefined
    d. Undefined

23. The term _____ can refer to an integer which is the square of some other integer, or an algebraic expression that can be factored as the square of some other expression.
    a. Perfect square0
    b. Thing
    c. Undefined
    d. Undefined

24. In geometry, a _____ is defined as a quadrilateral where all four of its angles are right angles.
    a. Rectangle0
    b. Thing
    c. Undefined
    d. Undefined

25. A _____ is any object propelled through space by the applicationp of a force.
    a. Thing
    b. Projectile0
    c. Undefined
    d. Undefined

26. _____ is the path a moving object follows through space.
    a. Projectile motion0
    b. Thing
    c. Undefined
    d. Undefined

27. Initial objects are also called _____, and terminal objects are also called final.
    a. Coterminal0
    b. Thing
    c. Undefined
    d. Undefined

28. A _____, scatter diagram or scatter graph is a graph used in statistics to visually display and relate two quantitative variables of a multidimensional data set by displaying the data as a collection of points, each having one coordinate on a horizontal and one on a vertical axis.
    a. Scatterplot0
    b. Thing
    c. Undefined
    d. Undefined

Chapter 3. Quadratic Functions and Equations

29. A _____ is a special kind of ratio, indicating a relationship between two measurements with different units, such as miles to gallons or cents to pounds.
   a. Thing
   b. Rate0
   c. Undefined
   d. Undefined

30. In regression analysis, _____, also known as ordinary _____ analysis is a method for linear regression that determines the values of unknown quantities in a statistical model by minimizing the sum of the residuals difference between the predicted and observed values squared.
   a. Least squares0
   b. Thing
   c. Undefined
   d. Undefined

31. _____ generally, is the synthesis of triose phospates and ultimately starch, glucose and other products from sunlight, carbon dioxide and water.
   a. Photosynthesis0
   b. Thing
   c. Undefined
   d. Undefined

32. _____ is a way of expressing a number as a fraction of 100 per cent meaning "per hundred".
   a. Thing
   b. Percent0
   c. Undefined
   d. Undefined

33. _____ is, or relates to, the _____ temperature scale .
   a. Celsius0
   b. Thing
   c. Undefined
   d. Undefined

34. In mathematics, there are several meanings of _____ depending on the subject.
   a. Thing
   b. Degree0
   c. Undefined
   d. Undefined

35. _____ is a physical property of a system that underlies the common notions of hot and cold; something that is hotter has the greater _____.
   a. Thing
   b. Temperature0
   c. Undefined
   d. Undefined

36. In the scientific method, an _____ (Latin: ex-+-periri, "of (or from) trying"), is a set of actions and observations, performed in the context of solving a particular problem or question, in order to support or falsify a hypothesis or research concerning phenomena.
   a. Thing
   b. Experiment0
   c. Undefined
   d. Undefined

37. In mathematics and the mathematical sciences, a _____ is a fixed, but possibly unspecified, value. This is in contrast to a variable, which is not fixed.
   a. Thing
   b. Constant0
   c. Undefined
   d. Undefined

38. One of the three formats applicable to a quadratic function is the _____ which is defined as $f = ax^2 + bx + c$.

Chapter 3. Quadratic Functions and Equations

a. Thing
c. Undefined

b. General form0
d. Undefined

39. _____ is a notation for writing numbers that is often used by scientists and mathematicians to make it easier to write large and small numbers.
    a. Scientific notation0
    c. Undefined
    b. Thing
    d. Undefined

40. In mathematics, a _____ function in the sense of algebraic geometry is an everywhere-defined, polynomial function on an algebraic variety V with values in the field K over which V is defined.
    a. Regular0
    c. Undefined
    b. Thing
    d. Undefined

41. _____ is a business term for the amount of money that a company receives from its activities in a given period, mostly from sales of products and/or services to customers
    a. Thing
    c. Undefined
    b. Revenue0
    d. Undefined

42. In geometry, an _____ of a triangle is a straight line through a vertex and perpendicular to (i.e. forming a right angle with) the opposite side or an extension of the opposite side.
    a. Concept
    c. Undefined
    b. Altitude0
    d. Undefined

43. _____ is defined as the rate of change or derivative with respect to time of velocity.
    a. Thing
    c. Undefined
    b. Acceleration0
    d. Undefined

44. _____ is the level of functional and/or metabolic efficiency of an organism at both the micro level.
    a. Health0
    c. Undefined
    b. Thing
    d. Undefined

45. In physics, _____ is an influence that may cause an object to accelerate. It may be experienced as a lift, a push, or a pull. The actual acceleration of the body is determined by the vector sum of all forces acting on it, known as net _____ or resultant _____.
    a. Force0
    c. Undefined
    b. Thing
    d. Undefined

46. A _____ is a type of bridge that has been created since ancient times as early as 100 AD.
    a. Thing
    c. Undefined
    b. Suspension bridge0
    d. Undefined

47. In geometry, the _____ of an object is a point in some sense in the middle of the object.
    a. Thing
    c. Undefined
    b. Center0
    d. Undefined

48. _____ means in succession or back-to-back

Chapter 3. Quadratic Functions and Equations

a. Thing
b. Consecutive0
c. Undefined
d. Undefined

49. In mathematics, a _____ is the end result of a division problem. It can also be expressed as the number of times the divisor divides into the dividend.
   a. Quotient0
   b. Thing
   c. Undefined
   d. Undefined

50. The function difference divided by the point difference is known as the _____
   a. Difference quotient0
   b. Thing
   c. Undefined
   d. Undefined

51. In Euclidean geometry, an _____ is a closed segment of a differentiable curve in the two-dimensional plane; for example, a circular _____ is a segment of a circle.
   a. Arc0
   b. Concept
   c. Undefined
   d. Undefined

52. In mathematics, a _____ is a polynomial equation of the second degree. The general form is $ax^2 + bx + c = 0$.
   a. Thing
   b. Quadratic equation0
   c. Undefined
   d. Undefined

53. A quadratic equation with real solutions, called roots, which may be real or complex, is given by the _____: $x = \frac{-b \pm \sqrt{b^2 - 4ac}}{2a}$.
   a. Thing
   b. Quadratic formula0
   c. Undefined
   d. Undefined

54. In mathematics, a _____ of a number x is a number r such that $r^2 = x$, or in words, a number r whose square (the result of multiplying the number by itself) is x.
   a. Square root0
   b. Thing
   c. Undefined
   d. Undefined

55. In mathematics, _____ is the decomposition of an object into a product of other objects, or factors, which when multiplied together give the original.
   a. Factoring0
   b. Thing
   c. Undefined
   d. Undefined

56. A _____ is an equation in which each term is either a constant or the product of a constant times the first power of a variable.
   a. Thing
   b. Linear equation0
   c. Undefined
   d. Undefined

57. In mathematics, a _____ of a complex-valued function f is a member x of the domain of f such that f(x) vanishes at x, that is, x : f (x) = 0.
   a. Root0
   b. Thing
   c. Undefined
   d. Undefined

Chapter 3. Quadratic Functions and Equations

58. _____ of a polynomial with real or complex coefficients is a certain expression in the coefficients of the polynomial which is equal to zero if and only if the polynomial has a multiple root i.e. a root with multiplicity greater than one in the complex numbers.
   a. Discriminant0
   b. Thing
   c. Undefined
   d. Undefined

59. A _____ is a negotiable instrument instructing a financial institution to pay a specific amount of a specific currency from a specific demand account held in the maker/depositor's name with that institution. Both the maker and payee may be natural persons or legal entities.
   a. Check0
   b. Thing
   c. Undefined
   d. Undefined

60. _____ is a state located in the Midwestern region of the United States of America.
   a. Thing
   b. Minnesota0
   c. Undefined
   d. Undefined

61. The _____ integers are all the integers from zero on upwards.
   a. Thing
   b. Nonnegative0
   c. Undefined
   d. Undefined

62. A _____ is a simplified and structured visual representation of concepts, ideas, constructions, relations, statistical data, anatomy etc used in all aspects of human activities to visualize and clarify the topic.
   a. Thing
   b. Diagram0
   c. Undefined
   d. Undefined

63. In mathematics, _____ expressions is used to reduce the expression into the lowest possible term.
   a. Thing
   b. Simplifying0
   c. Undefined
   d. Undefined

64. _____ forms part of thinking. Considered the most complex of all intellectual functions, _____ has been defined as higher-order cognitive process that requires the modulation and control of more routine or fundamental skills.
   a. Thing
   b. Problem solving0
   c. Undefined
   d. Undefined

65. The _____ of a solid object is the three-dimensional concept of how much space it occupies, often quantified numerically.
   a. Thing
   b. Volume0
   c. Undefined
   d. Undefined

66. In mathematics, a subset of Euclidean space R^n is called _____ if it is closed and bounded.
   a. Compact0
   b. Thing
   c. Undefined
   d. Undefined

67. In finance and economics, _____ is the process of finding the present value of an amount of cash at some future date, and along with compounding cash forms the basis of time value of money calculations.

Chapter 3. Quadratic Functions and Equations

   a. Discount0
   b. Thing
   c. Undefined
   d. Undefined

68. _____ the expected value of a random variable displays the average or central value of the variable. It is a summary value of the distribution of the variable.
   a. Thing
   b. Determining0
   c. Undefined
   d. Undefined

69. Equivalence is the condition of being _____ or essentially equal.
   a. Equivalent0
   b. Thing
   c. Undefined
   d. Undefined

70. The deductive-nomological model is a formalized view of scientific _____ in natural language.
   a. Explanation0
   b. Thing
   c. Undefined
   d. Undefined

71. In mathematics, an _____ number is any real number that is not a rational number- that is, it is a number which cannot be expressed as a fraction m/n, where m and n are integers.
   a. Thing
   b. Irrational0
   c. Undefined
   d. Undefined

72. In mathematics, an _____ is any real number that is not a rational number ¡ª that is, it is a number which cannot be expressed as m/n, where m and n are integers.
   a. Thing
   b. Irrational number0
   c. Undefined
   d. Undefined

73. In mathematics, _____ are any real number that is not a rational number ¡ª that is, it is a number which cannot be expressed as m/n, where m and n are integers.
   a. Thing
   b. Irrational numbers0
   c. Undefined
   d. Undefined

74. _____ of an object is its speed in a particular direction.
   a. Velocity0
   b. Thing
   c. Undefined
   d. Undefined

75. In mathematics, the concept of a _____ tries to capture the intuitive idea of a geometrical one-dimensional and continuous object. A simple example is the circle.
   a. Curve0
   b. Thing
   c. Undefined
   d. Undefined

76. In mathematics, _____ are the intuitive idea of a geometrical one-dimensional and continuous object.
   a. Thing
   b. Curves0
   c. Undefined
   d. Undefined

Chapter 3. Quadratic Functions and Equations

77. In classical geometry, a _____ of a circle or sphere is any line segment from its center to its boundary. By extension, the _____ of a circle or sphere is the length of any such segment. The _____ is half the diameter. In science and engineering the term _____ of curvature is commonly used as a synonym for _____.
    a. Radius0
    b. Thing
    c. Undefined
    d. Undefined

78. An _____ is a collection of two not necessarily distinct objects, one of which is distinguished as the first coordinate and the other as the second coordinate.
    a. Thing
    b. Ordered pair0
    c. Undefined
    d. Undefined

79. In mathematics, the conjugate _____ or adjoint matrix of an m-by-n matrix A with complex entries is the n-by-m matrix A* obtained from A by taking the transpose and then taking the complex conjugate of each entry.
    a. Thing
    b. Pairs0
    c. Undefined
    d. Undefined

80. _____ is the ability to hold, receive or absorb, or a measure thereof, similar to the concept of volume.
    a. Capacity0
    b. Concept
    c. Undefined
    d. Undefined

81. _____ is a mathematical science pertaining to the collection, analysis, interpretation or explanation, and presentation of data. It is applicable to a wide variety of academic disciplines, from the physical and social sciences to the humanities.
    a. Thing
    b. Statistics0
    c. Undefined
    d. Undefined

82. A _____ is a unit of length, usually used to measure distance, in a number of different systems, including Imperial units, United States customary units and Norwegian/Swedish mil. Its size can vary from system to system, but in each is between 1 and 10 kilometers. In contemporary English contexts _____ refers to either:
    a. Mile0
    b. Thing
    c. Undefined
    d. Undefined

83. _____ is a unit of speed, expressing the number of international miles covered per hour.
    a. Thing
    b. Miles per hour0
    c. Undefined
    d. Undefined

84. A _____ is a function that assigns a number to subsets of a given set.
    a. Measure0
    b. Thing
    c. Undefined
    d. Undefined

85. Compass and straightedge or ruler-and-compass _____ is the _____ of lengths or angles using only an idealized ruler and compass.
    a. Construction0
    b. Thing
    c. Undefined
    d. Undefined

Chapter 3. Quadratic Functions and Equations

86. In mathematics, a _____ is a quadric surface, with the following equation in Cartesian coordinates: $(x/_a)^2 + (y/_b)^2 = 1$.
   a. Cylinder0
   b. Thing
   c. Undefined
   d. Undefined

87. A _____ is a set of possible values that a variable can take on in order to satisfy a given set of conditions, which may include equations and inequalities.
   a. Thing
   b. Solution set0
   c. Undefined
   d. Undefined

88. In mathematics, an _____ is a statement about the relative size or order of two objects.
   a. Inequality0
   b. Thing
   c. Undefined
   d. Undefined

89. Two mathematical objects are equal if and only if they are precisely the same in every way. This defines a binary relation, _____, denoted by the sign of _____ "=" in such a way that the statement "x = y" means that x and y are equal.
   a. Thing
   b. Equality0
   c. Undefined
   d. Undefined

90. In mathematics, an inequality is a statement about the relative size or order of two objects. For example 14 > 10, or 14 is _____ 10.
   a. Greater than0
   b. Thing
   c. Undefined
   d. Undefined

91. Mathematical _____ is used to represent ideas.
   a. Notation0
   b. Thing
   c. Undefined
   d. Undefined

92. Any point where a graph makes contact with an coordinate axis is called an _____ of the graph
   a. Intercept0
   b. Thing
   c. Undefined
   d. Undefined

93. In elementary algebra, an _____ is a set that contains every real number between two indicated numbers and may contain the two numbers themselves.
   a. Interval0
   b. Thing
   c. Undefined
   d. Undefined

94. _____ is the notation in which permitted values for a variable are expressed as ranging over a certain interval; "5 < x < 9" is an example of the application of _____.
   a. Interval notation0
   b. Thing
   c. Undefined
   d. Undefined

95. In mathematics and more specifically set theory, the _____ set is the unique set which contains no elements.

Chapter 3. Quadratic Functions and Equations

    a. Empty0
    b. Thing
    c. Undefined
    d. Undefined

96. A _____ is a one-dimensional picture in which the integers are shown as specially-marked points evenly spaced on a line.
    a. Thing
    b. Number line0
    c. Undefined
    d. Undefined

97. In mathematics, two sets are said to be _____ if they have no element in common. For example, {1, 2, 3} and {4, 5, 6} are sets which are _____.
    a. Thing
    b. Disjoint0
    c. Undefined
    d. Undefined

98. _____ are a measure of time.
    a. Thing
    b. Minutes0
    c. Undefined
    d. Undefined

99. _____ is mass m per unit volume V.
    a. Thing
    b. Density0
    c. Undefined
    d. Undefined

100. The _____ or kilogramme is the SI base unit of mass. It is defined as being equal to the mass of the international prototype of the _____.
    a. Thing
    b. Kilogram0
    c. Undefined
    d. Undefined

101. The metre (or _____, see spelling differences) is a measure of length. It is the basic unit of length in the metric system and in the International System of Units (SI), used around the world for general and scientific purposes.
    a. Concept
    b. Meter0
    c. Undefined
    d. Undefined

102. In geometry, a _____ (Greek words diairo = divide and metro = measure) of a circle is any straight line segment that passes through the centre and whose endpoints are on the circular boundary, or, in more modern usage, the length of such a line segment. When using the word in the more modern sense, one speaks of the _____ rather than a _____, because all diameters of a circle have the same length. This length is twice the radius. The _____ of a circle is also the longest chord that the circle has.
    a. Thing
    b. Diameter0
    c. Undefined
    d. Undefined

103. _____ is a kind of property which exists as magnitude or multitude. It is among the basic classes of things along with quality, substance, change, and relation.
    a. Amount0
    b. Thing
    c. Undefined
    d. Undefined

104. In Euclidean geometry, a _____ is moving every point a constant distance in a specified direction.

Chapter 3. Quadratic Functions and Equations

    a. Translation0
    b. Concept
    c. Undefined
    d. Undefined

105. In astronomy, geography, geometry and related sciences and contexts, a plane is said to be _____ at a given point if it is locally perpendicular to the gradient of the gravity field, i.e., with the direction of the gravitational force at that point.
    a. Horizontal0
    b. Thing
    c. Undefined
    d. Undefined

106. Mathematical _____ are the wide variety of ways to capture an abstract mathematical concept or relationship.
    a. Representations0
    b. Thing
    c. Undefined
    d. Undefined

107. The _____ of measurement are a globally standardized and modernized form of the metric system.
    a. Units0
    b. Thing
    c. Undefined
    d. Undefined

108. In mathematics, an _____, isometric isomorphism or congruence mapping is a distance-preserving isomorphism between metric spaces.
    a. Isometry0
    b. Thing
    c. Undefined
    d. Undefined

109. A _____ is a symbolic representation denoting a quantity or expression. It often represents an "unknown" quantity that has the potential to change.
    a. Thing
    b. Variable0
    c. Undefined
    d. Undefined

110. In mathematics, a _____ in elementary terms is any of a variety of different functions from geometry, such as rotations, reflections and translations.
    a. Transformation0
    b. Thing
    c. Undefined
    d. Undefined

111. In mathematics, the _____ f is the collection of all ordered pairs . In particular, graph means the graphical representation of this collection, in the form of a curve or surface, together with axes, etc. Graphing on a Cartesian plane is sometimes referred to as curve sketching.
    a. Thing
    b. Graph of a function0
    c. Undefined
    d. Undefined

112. In mathematics, a _____ (also spelled reflexion) is a map that transforms an object into its mirror image.
    a. Reflection0
    b. Concept
    c. Undefined
    d. Undefined

113. In geographic information systems, a _____ comprises an entity with a geographic location, typically determined by points, arcs, or polygons. Carriageways and cadastres exemplify _____ data.
    a. Thing
    b. Feature0
    c. Undefined
    d. Undefined

Chapter 3. Quadratic Functions and Equations

114. A _____ is a unit of length in the metric system, equal to one thousand metres, the current SI base unit of length
   a. Kilometer0
   b. Thing
   c. Undefined
   d. Undefined

115. A _____ is a landform that extends above the surrounding terrain in a limited area. A _____ is generally steeper than a hill, but there is no universally accepted standard definition for the height of a _____ or a hill although a _____ usually has an identifiable summit.
   a. Mountain0
   b. Thing
   c. Undefined
   d. Undefined

116. In mathematics, _____ is a part of the set theoretic notion of function.
   a. Image0
   b. Thing
   c. Undefined
   d. Undefined

117. In mathematics, an _____, mean, or central tendency of a data set refers to a measure of the "middle" or "expected" value of the data set.
   a. Average0
   b. Concept
   c. Undefined
   d. Undefined

118. _____, usually denoted symbolically by the Greek letter phi, ϕ, gives the location of a place on Earth north or south of the equator. _____ is an angular measurement in degrees (marked with °) ranging from 0° at the Equator (low _____) to 90° at the poles (90° N for the North Pole or 90° S for the South Pole; high _____). The complementary angle of a _____ is called the colatitude.
   a. Thing
   b. Latitude0
   c. Undefined
   d. Undefined

119. In mathematics, a _____ is an ordered list of objects. Like a set, it contains members, also called elements or terms, and the number of terms is called the length of the _____. Unlike a set, order matters, and the exact same elements can appear multiple times at different positions in the _____.
   a. Thing
   b. Sequence0
   c. Undefined
   d. Undefined

120. Acid _____ ratio measures the ability of a company to use its near cash or quick assets to immediately extinguish its current liabilities.
   a. Thing
   b. Test0
   c. Undefined
   d. Undefined

121. A _____ is a statement or claimt that a particular event will occur in the future in more certain terms than a forecast.
   a. Thing
   b. Prediction0
   c. Undefined
   d. Undefined

122. The _____ is the total number of human beings alive on the planet Earth at a given time.
   a. Thing
   b. World population0
   c. Undefined
   d. Undefined

Chapter 3. Quadratic Functions and Equations

123. In sociology and biology a _____ is the collection of people or organisms of a particular species living in a given geographic area or space, usually measured by a census.
   a. Thing
   b. Population0
   c. Undefined
   d. Undefined

124. In business, particularly accounting, a _____ is the time intervals that the accounts, statement, payments, or other calculations cover.
   a. Thing
   b. Period0
   c. Undefined
   d. Undefined

125. _____ is the state of being greater than any finite real or natural number, however large.
   a. Thing
   b. Infinite0
   c. Undefined
   d. Undefined

126. _____ (March 14, 1879 - April 18, 1955) was a German-born theoretical physicist who is best known for his theory of relativity and specifically mass-energy equivalence, $E = mc^2$.
   a. Albert Einstein0
   b. Person
   c. Undefined
   d. Undefined

127. In mathematics, a _____ is a demonstration that, assuming certain axioms, some statement is necessarily true.
   a. Proof0
   b. Thing
   c. Undefined
   d. Undefined

128. Mathematical _____ are demonstrations that, assuming certain axioms, some statement is necessarily true.
   a. Thing
   b. Proofs0
   c. Undefined
   d. Undefined

129. An _____ is any starting assumption from which other statements are logically derived
   a. Thing
   b. Axiom0
   c. Undefined
   d. Undefined

130. In mathematics, a _____ is a statement that can be proved on the basis of explicitly stated or previously agreed assumptions.
   a. Thing
   b. Theorem0
   c. Undefined
   d. Undefined

131. A central concept in science and the scientific method is that all evidence must be _____, or empirically based, that is, dependent on evidence or consequences that are observable by the senses.
   a. Thing
   b. Empirical0
   c. Undefined
   d. Undefined

132. In statistics, a _____ measure is one which is measuring what is supposed to measure.
   a. Valid0
   b. Thing
   c. Undefined
   d. Undefined

133. In mathematics, the word _____ is used informally to refer to certain distinct bodies of knowledge about mathematics.
   a. Theoretical0
   b. Thing
   c. Undefined
   d. Undefined

134. In abstract algebra, a _____ is an algebraic structure, a collection of elements and operations on them obeying defining axioms, that captures essential properties of both set operations and logic operations. Specifically, it deals with the set operations of intersection, union, complement; and the logic operations of AND, OR, NOT.
   a. Boolean algebra0
   b. Thing
   c. Undefined
   d. Undefined

135. In mathematics, a _____ is a number in the form of a + bi where a and b are real numbers, and i is the imaginary unit, with the property $i^2 = -1$. The real number a is called the real part of the _____, and the real number b is the imaginary part.
   a. Thing
   b. Complex number0
   c. Undefined
   d. Undefined

136. _____, Greek for "knowledge of nature," is the branch of science concerned with the discovery and characterization of universal laws which govern matter, energy, space, and time.
   a. Physics0
   b. Thing
   c. Undefined
   d. Undefined

137. In colloquial usage, a _____ is "a rough or fragmented geometric shape that can be subdivided in parts, each of which is, at least approximately, a reduced-size copy of the whole."
   a. Fractal0
   b. Concept
   c. Undefined
   d. Undefined

Chapter 4. Nonlinear Functions and Equations

1. _____ is a synonym for information.
   - a. Thing
   - b. Data0
   - c. Undefined
   - d. Undefined

2. The word _____ comes from the Latin word linearis, which means created by lines.
   - a. Thing
   - b. Linear0
   - c. Undefined
   - d. Undefined

3. A _____ is a first degree polynomial mathematical function of the form: $f(x) = mx + b$ where m and b are real constants and x is a real variable.
   - a. Thing
   - b. Linear function0
   - c. Undefined
   - d. Undefined

4. The mathematical concept of a _____ expresses the intuitive idea of deterministic dependence between two quantities, one of which is viewed as primary and the other as secondary. A _____ then is a way to associate a unique output for each input of a specified type, for example, a real number or an element of a given set.
   - a. Thing
   - b. Function0
   - c. Undefined
   - d. Undefined

5. In mathematics, there are several meanings of _____ depending on the subject.
   - a. Thing
   - b. Degree0
   - c. Undefined
   - d. Undefined

6. In mathematics, a _____ is an expression that is constructed from one or more variables and constants, using only the operations of addition, subtraction, multiplication, and constant positive whole number exponents. is a _____. Note in particular that division by an expression containing a variable is not in general allowed in polynomials. [1]
   - a. Polynomial0
   - b. Thing
   - c. Undefined
   - d. Undefined

7. _____ is a physical property of a system that underlies the common notions of hot and cold; something that is hotter has the greater _____.
   - a. Thing
   - b. Temperature0
   - c. Undefined
   - d. Undefined

8. A _____ function is a function for which, intuitively, small changes in the input result in small changes in the output.
   - a. Continuous0
   - b. Event
   - c. Undefined
   - d. Undefined

9. In mathematics, a _____ may be described informally as a number that can be given by an infinite decimal representation.
   - a. Real number0
   - b. Thing
   - c. Undefined
   - d. Undefined

10. In mathematics, a _____ of a k-place relation $L \subseteq X_1 \times \ldots \times X_k$ is one of the sets X_j, $1 \leq j \leq k$. In the special case where k = 2 and $L \subseteq X_1 \times X_2$ is a function $L : X_1 \to X_2$, it is conventional to refer to X_1 as the _____ of the function and to refer to X_2 as the codomain of the function.

a. Domain0
b. Thing
c. Undefined
d. Undefined

11. A _____ is a symbolic representation denoting a quantity or expression. It often represents an "unknown" quantity that has the potential to change.
    a. Thing
    b. Variable0
    c. Undefined
    d. Undefined

12. The _____ integers are all the integers from zero on upwards.
    a. Nonnegative0
    b. Thing
    c. Undefined
    d. Undefined

13. In mathematics, a _____ is a constant multiplicative factor of a certain object. The object can be such things as a variable, a vector, a function, etc. For example, the _____ of $9x^2$ is 9.
    a. Thing
    b. Coefficient0
    c. Undefined
    d. Undefined

14. _____ systems represent systems whose behavior is not expressible as a sum of the behaviors of its descriptors.
    a. Nonlinear0
    b. Thing
    c. Undefined
    d. Undefined

15. _____ is a branch of mathematics concerning the study of structure, relation and quantity.
    a. Algebra0
    b. Concept
    c. Undefined
    d. Undefined

16. _____ is the symbold used to indicate the nth root of a number
    a. Radical0
    b. Thing
    c. Undefined
    d. Undefined

17. In mathematics, _____ are used to indicate the square root of a number.
    a. Radicals0
    b. Thing
    c. Undefined
    d. Undefined

18. A _____ is a quantity that denotes the proportional amount or magnitude of one quantity relative to another.
    a. Ratio0
    b. Thing
    c. Undefined
    d. Undefined

19. In mathematics, the _____ (or modulus) of a real number is its numerical value without regard to its sign.
    a. Thing
    b. Absolute value0
    c. Undefined
    d. Undefined

20. In mathematics, the _____ f is the collection of all ordered pairs . In particular, graph means the graphical representation of this collection, in the form of a curve or surface, together with axes, etc. Graphing on a Cartesian plane is sometimes referred to as curve sketching.

Chapter 4. Nonlinear Functions and Equations   57

   a. Thing
   c. Undefined
   b. Graph of a function0
   d. Undefined

21. A _____ is a one-dimensional picture in which the integers are shown as specially-marked points evenly spaced on a line.
   a. Thing
   c. Undefined
   b. Number line0
   d. Undefined

22. In elementary algebra, an _____ is a set that contains every real number between two indicated numbers and may contain the two numbers themselves.
   a. Interval0
   c. Undefined
   b. Thing
   d. Undefined

23. _____ the expected value of a random variable displays the average or central value of the variable. It is a summary value of the distribution of the variable.
   a. Determining0
   c. Undefined
   b. Thing
   d. Undefined

24. Mathematical _____ is used to represent ideas.
   a. Thing
   c. Undefined
   b. Notation0
   d. Undefined

25. _____ is the notation in which permitted values for a variable are expressed as ranging over a certain interval; "5 < x < 9" is an example of the application of _____.
   a. Interval notation0
   c. Undefined
   b. Thing
   d. Undefined

26. In mathematics, the _____ is a conic section generated by the intersection of a right circular conical surface and a plane parallel to a generating straight line of that surface. It can also be defined as locus of points in a plane which are equidistant from a given point.
   a. Thing
   c. Undefined
   b. Parabola0
   d. Undefined

27. In linear algebra, the _____ of an n-by-n square matrix A is defined to be the sum of the elements on the main diagonal of A,
   a. Thing
   c. Undefined
   b. Trace0
   d. Undefined

28. In geometry, a _____ is a special kind of point, usually a corner of a polygon, polyhedron, or higher dimensional polytope. In the geometry of curves a _____ is a point of where the first derivative of curvature is zero. In graph theory, a _____ is the fundamental unit out of which graphs are formed
   a. Vertex0
   c. Undefined
   b. Thing
   d. Undefined

Chapter 4. Nonlinear Functions and Equations

29. in mathematics, maxima and minima, known collectively as _____, are the largest value maximum or smallest value minimum, that a function takes in a point either within a given neighborhood or on the function domain in its entirety global extremum.
    a. Thing
    b. Extrema0
    c. Undefined
    d. Undefined

30. In mathematics, maxima and minima, known collectively as extrema, are the largest value maximum or smallest value minimum, that a function takes in a point either within a given neighborhood local _____ or on the function domain in its entirety global _____.
    a. Extremum0
    b. Thing
    c. Undefined
    d. Undefined

31. A real-valued function f defined on the real line is said to have a _____ point at the point x∗, if there exists some ε > 0, such that f when x − x∗ < ε.
    a. Thing
    b. Local maximum0
    c. Undefined
    d. Undefined

32. _____ is a kind of property which exists as magnitude or multitude. It is among the basic classes of things along with quality, substance, change, and relation.
    a. Thing
    b. Amount0
    c. Undefined
    d. Undefined

33. The _____ of a solid object is the three-dimensional concept of how much space it occupies, often quantified numerically.
    a. Volume0
    b. Thing
    c. Undefined
    d. Undefined

34. The term _____ refers to the largest and the smallest element of a set.
    a. Thing
    b. Extreme value0
    c. Undefined
    d. Undefined

35. In mathematics, _____ is a part of the set theoretic notion of function.
    a. Thing
    b. Image0
    c. Undefined
    d. Undefined

36. The _____ of a ring R is defined to be the smallest positive integer n such that n a = 0, for all a in R.
    a. Characteristic0
    b. Thing
    c. Undefined
    d. Undefined

37. _____ are functions which satisfy particular symmetry relations, with respect to taking additive inverses.
    a. Even function0
    b. Thing
    c. Undefined
    d. Undefined

38. _____ means "constancy", i.e. if something retains a certain feature even after we change a way of looking at it, then it is symmetric.

Chapter 4. Nonlinear Functions and Equations

    a. Symmetry0
    b. Thing
    c. Undefined
    d. Undefined

39. A _____ is 360° or 2δ radians.
    a. Turn0
    b. Thing
    c. Undefined
    d. Undefined

40. In mathematics, the _____ of a coordinate system is the point where the axes of the system intersect.
    a. Origin0
    b. Thing
    c. Undefined
    d. Undefined

41. _____ has many meanings, most of which simply .
    a. Thing
    b. Power0
    c. Undefined
    d. Undefined

42. In mathematics, _____ and odd functions are functions which satisfy particular symmetry relations, with respect to taking additive inverses.
    a. Even functions0
    b. Thing
    c. Undefined
    d. Undefined

43. In common philosophical language, a proposition or _____, is the content of an assertion, that is, it is true-or-false and defined by the meaning of a particular piece of language.
    a. Statement0
    b. Concept
    c. Undefined
    d. Undefined

44. A _____ is a three-dimensional solid object bounded by six square faces, facets, or sides, with three meeting at each vertex.
    a. Thing
    b. Cube0
    c. Undefined
    d. Undefined

45. A _____ of a number is a number a such that $a^3 = x$.
    a. Thing
    b. Cube root0
    c. Undefined
    d. Undefined

46. In mathematics, a _____ of a complex-valued function f is a member x of the domain of f such that f(x) vanishes at x, that is, x : f (x) = 0.
    a. Thing
    b. Root0
    c. Undefined
    d. Undefined

47. _____ are the basic objects of study in graph theory. Informally speaking, a graph is a set of objects called points, nodes, or vertices connected by links called lines or edges.
    a. Thing
    b. Graphs0
    c. Undefined
    d. Undefined

48. A _____ is a function for which, intuitively, small changes in the input result in small changes in the output.

a. Continuous function0
b. Event
c. Undefined
d. Undefined

49. In Euclidean geometry, a _____ is moving every point a constant distance in a specified direction.
   a. Translation0
   b. Concept
   c. Undefined
   d. Undefined

50. _____, usually denoted symbolically by the Greek letter phi, Î¦, gives the location of a place on Earth north or south of the equator. _____ is an angular measurement in degrees (marked with Â°) ranging from 0Â° at the Equator (low _____) to 90Â° at the poles (90Â° N for the North Pole or 90Â° S for the South Pole; high _____). The complementary angle of a _____ is called the colatitude.
   a. Latitude0
   b. Thing
   c. Undefined
   d. Undefined

51. In mathematics, an _____, mean, or central tendency of a data set refers to a measure of the "middle" or "expected" value of the data set.
   a. Concept
   b. Average0
   c. Undefined
   d. Undefined

52. _____ is a temperature scale named after the German physicist Daniel Gabriel _____ , who proposed it in 1724.
   a. Fahrenheit0
   b. Thing
   c. Undefined
   d. Undefined

53. _____ is a state located in the southern and southwestern regions of the United States of America.
   a. Texas0
   b. Thing
   c. Undefined
   d. Undefined

54. _____ is a measure of difference for interval and ratio variables between the observed value and the mean.
   a. Thing
   b. Deviation0
   c. Undefined
   d. Undefined

55. A _____ is any object propelled through space by the applicationp of a force.
   a. Projectile0
   b. Thing
   c. Undefined
   d. Undefined

56. _____ of an object is its speed in a particular direction.
   a. Thing
   b. Velocity0
   c. Undefined
   d. Undefined

57. In geometry, a _____ is defined as a quadrilateral where all four of its angles are right angles.
   a. Thing
   b. Rectangle0
   c. Undefined
   d. Undefined

Chapter 4. Nonlinear Functions and Equations

58. A _____ is a unit of length, usually used to measure distance, in a number of different systems, including Imperial units, United States customary units and Norwegian/Swedish mil. Its size can vary from system to system, but in each is between 1 and 10 kilometers. In contemporary English contexts _____ refers to either:
   a. Thing
   b. Mile0
   c. Undefined
   d. Undefined

59. _____ is a unit of speed, expressing the number of international miles covered per hour.
   a. Thing
   b. Miles per hour0
   c. Undefined
   d. Undefined

60. _____ are a measure of time.
   a. Minutes0
   b. Thing
   c. Undefined
   d. Undefined

61. A _____ was a citizen of Babylonia, named for its capital city, Babylon, which was an ancient state in the south part of Mesopotamia (in modern Iraq), combining the territories of Sumer and Akkad.
   a. Place
   b. Babylonian0
   c. Undefined
   d. Undefined

62. A _____, scatter diagram or scatter graph is a graph used in statistics to visually display and relate two quantitative variables of a multidimensional data set by displaying the data as a collection of points, each having one coordinate on a horizontal and one on a vertical axis.
   a. Scatterplot0
   b. Thing
   c. Undefined
   d. Undefined

63. An _____ is a combination of numbers, operators, grouping symbols and/or free variables and bound variables arranged in a meaningful way which can be evaluated..
   a. Thing
   b. Expression0
   c. Undefined
   d. Undefined

64. In astronomy, geography, geometry and related sciences and contexts, a plane is said to be _____ at a given point if it is locally perpendicular to the gradient of the gravity field, i.e., with the direction of the gravitational force at that point.
   a. Thing
   b. Horizontal0
   c. Undefined
   d. Undefined

65. A _____ is a polynomial function of the form $f(x) = ax^2 + bx + c$, where a, b, c are real numbers and a , 0.
   a. Quadratic function0
   b. Event
   c. Undefined
   d. Undefined

66. _____ is a function of the form
   a. Cubic function0
   b. Thing
   c. Undefined
   d. Undefined

67. In mathematics and elsewhere, the adjective _____ means fourth order, such as the function $x4$. A _____ number is a number which equals the fourth power of an integer.

Chapter 4. Nonlinear Functions and Equations

    a. Quartic0   b. Thing
    c. Undefined   d. Undefined

68. A _____ is a polynomial function with a degree of four. It has the same limit when the argument goes to positive or negative infinity.
    a. Quartic function0   b. Thing
    c. Undefined   d. Undefined

69. A _____ is a set of numbers that designate location in a given reference system, such as x,y in a planar _____ system or an x,y,z in a three-dimensional _____ system.
    a. Coordinate0   b. Thing
    c. Undefined   d. Undefined

70. A _____ defined function $f(x)$ of a real variable x is a function whose definition is given differently on disjoint subsets of its domain.
    a. Thing   b. Piecewise0
    c. Undefined   d. Undefined

71. In a mathematical proof or a syllogism, a _____ is a statement that is the logical consequence of preceding statements.
    a. Concept   b. Conclusion0
    c. Undefined   d. Undefined

72. A _____ is a special kind of ratio, indicating a relationship between two measurements with different units, such as miles to gallons or cents to pounds.
    a. Thing   b. Rate0
    c. Undefined   d. Undefined

73. In mathematics and the mathematical sciences, a _____ is a fixed, but possibly unspecified, value. This is in contrast to a variable, which is not fixed.
    a. Constant0   b. Thing
    c. Undefined   d. Undefined

74. A quadratic equation with real solutions, called roots, which may be real or complex, is given by the _____: $x = \frac{-b \pm \sqrt{b^2 - 4ac}}{2a}$.
    a. Thing   b. Quadratic formula0
    c. Undefined   d. Undefined

75. In mathematics, a _____ is a mathematical statement which appears likely to be true, but has not been formally proven to be true under the rules of mathematical logic.
    a. Concept   b. Conjecture0
    c. Undefined   d. Undefined

76. In mathematics, a _____ is the end result of a division problem. It can also be expressed as the number of times the divisor divides into the dividend.

Chapter 4. Nonlinear Functions and Equations

 a. Quotient0   b. Thing
 c. Undefined   d. Undefined

77. In mathematics, the concept of a _____ tries to capture the intuitive idea of a geometrical one-dimensional and continuous object. A simple example is the circle.
 a. Thing   b. Curve0
 c. Undefined   d. Undefined

78. In mathematics, _____ are the intuitive idea of a geometrical one-dimensional and continuous object.
 a. Curves0   b. Thing
 c. Undefined   d. Undefined

79. Transport or _____ is the movement of people and goods from one place to another.
 a. Transportation0   b. Thing
 c. Undefined   d. Undefined

80. _____ refers to all non-domesticated plants, animals, and other organisms.
 a. Thing   b. Wildlife0
 c. Undefined   d. Undefined

81. The _____, the average in everyday English, which is also called the arithmetic _____ (and is distinguished from the geometric _____ or harmonic _____). The average is also called the sample _____. The expected value of a random variable, which is also called the population _____.
 a. Thing   b. Mean0
 c. Undefined   d. Undefined

82. In mathematics, maxima and _____, known collectively as extrema, are points in the domain of a function at which the function takes a largest value .
 a. Minima0   b. Thing
 c. Undefined   d. Undefined

83. A _____ is a polynomial equation in which the greatest exponent on the independent variable is five.
 a. Quintic equation0   b. Thing
 c. Undefined   d. Undefined

84. Leonhard _____ was a pioneering Swiss mathematician and physicist, who spent most of his life in Russia and Germany.
 a. Euler0   b. Person
 c. Undefined   d. Undefined

85. In business, particularly accounting, a _____ is the time intervals that the accounts, statement, payments, or other calculations cover.
 a. Thing   b. Period0
 c. Undefined   d. Undefined

Chapter 4. Nonlinear Functions and Equations

86. In sociology and biology a _____ is the collection of people or organisms of a particular species living in a given geographic area or space, usually measured by a census.
   a. Population0
   b. Thing
   c. Undefined
   d. Undefined

87. In mathematics, _____ is the decomposition of an object into a product of other objects, or factors, which when multiplied together give the original.
   a. Factoring0
   b. Thing
   c. Undefined
   d. Undefined

88. In mathematics, a _____ is a particular kind of polynomial, having just one term.
   a. Monomial0
   b. Thing
   c. Undefined
   d. Undefined

89. A _____ is a numeral used to indicate a count. The most common use of the word today is to name the part of a fraction that tells the number or count of equal parts.
   a. Thing
   b. Numerator0
   c. Undefined
   d. Undefined

90. In mathematics, a _____ can mean either an element of the set {1, 2, 3, ...} (i.e the positive integers or the counting numbers) or an element of the set {0, 1, 2, 3, ...} (i.e. the non-negative integers).
   a. Natural number0
   b. Thing
   c. Undefined
   d. Undefined

91. In elementary algebra, a _____ is a polynomial with two terms: the sum of two monomials. It is the simplest kind of polynomial except for a monomial.
   a. Thing
   b. Binomial0
   c. Undefined
   d. Undefined

92. A _____ is the part of the dividend that is left over when the dividend is not evenly divisible by the divisor.
   a. Remainder0
   b. Thing
   c. Undefined
   d. Undefined

93. _____ is a payment made by a company to its shareholders
   a. Thing
   b. Dividend0
   c. Undefined
   d. Undefined

94. In mathematics, a _____ of an integer n, also called a factor of n, is an integer which evenly divides n without leaving a remainder.
   a. Divisor0
   b. Thing
   c. Undefined
   d. Undefined

95. A _____ is a negotiable instrument instructing a financial institution to pay a specific amount of a specific currency from a specific demand account held in the maker/depositor's name with that institution. Both the maker and payee may be natural persons or legal entities.

a. Check0
b. Thing
c. Undefined
d. Undefined

96. In mathematics, _____ is an elementary arithmetic operation. When one of the numbers is a whole number, _____ is the repeated sum of the other number.
   a. Multiplication0
   b. Thing
   c. Undefined
   d. Undefined

97. In mathematics, _____ allows the rapid division of any polynomial by a binomial of the form x − r. It was described by Paolo Ruffini in 1809. _____ is a special case of long division when the divisor is a linear factor.
   a. Thing
   b. Ruffini's rule0
   c. Undefined
   d. Undefined

98. Equivalence is the condition of being _____ or essentially equal.
   a. Thing
   b. Equivalent0
   c. Undefined
   d. Undefined

99. In arithmetic, _____ is a procedure for calculating the division of one integer, called the dividend, by another integer called the divisor, to produce a result called the quotient.
   a. Thing
   b. Long division0
   c. Undefined
   d. Undefined

100. In mathematics, a matrix can be thought of as each row or _____ being a vector. Hence, a space formed by row vectors or _____ vectors are said to be a row space or a _____ space.
   a. Concept
   b. Column0
   c. Undefined
   d. Undefined

101. In mathematics, an inequality is a statement about the relative size or order of two objects. For example 14 > 10, or 14 is _____ 10.
   a. Thing
   b. Greater than0
   c. Undefined
   d. Undefined

102. In mathematics, computing, linguistics, and related disciplines, an _____ is a finite list of well-defined instructions for accomplishing some task which, given an initial state, will terminate in a defined end-state.
   a. Concept
   b. Algorithm0
   c. Undefined
   d. Undefined

103. The _____ is a theorem in mathematics which precisely expresses the outcome of the usual process of division of integers. The name is something of a misnomer, as it is a theorem, not an algorithm, i.e. a well-defined procedure for achieving a specific task — although the _____ can be used to find the greatest common divisor of two integers.
   a. Division Algorithm0
   b. Thing
   c. Undefined
   d. Undefined

104. _____ in algebra is an application of polynomial long division.

Chapter 4. Nonlinear Functions and Equations

    a. Remainder theorem0
    b. Thing
    c. Undefined
    d. Undefined

105. In mathematics, a _____ is a statement that can be proved on the basis of explicitly stated or previously agreed assumptions.
    a. Thing
    b. Theorem0
    c. Undefined
    d. Undefined

106. The _____ is a theorem for finding out the factors of a polynomial.
    a. Factor theorem0
    b. Thing
    c. Undefined
    d. Undefined

107. In mathematics, factorization (British English: factorisation) or factoring is the decomposition of an object (for example, a number, a polynomial, or a matrix) into a product of other objects, or _____, which when multiplied together give the original.
    a. Thing
    b. Factors0
    c. Undefined
    d. Undefined

108. The _____ of a member of a multiset is how many memberships in the multiset it has.
    a. Thing
    b. Multiplicity0
    c. Undefined
    d. Undefined

109. _____ is the mathematical action of repeatedly adding or subtracting one, usually to find out how many objects there are or to set aside a desired number of objects.
    a. Counting0
    b. Thing
    c. Undefined
    d. Undefined

110. The _____ are the only integral domain whose positive elements are well-ordered, and in which order is preserved by addition. Like the natural numbers, the _____ form a countably infinite set. The set of all _____ is usually denoted in mathematics by a boldface Z .
    a. Thing
    b. Integers0
    c. Undefined
    d. Undefined

111. A _____ of a number is the product of that number with any integer.
    a. Multiple0
    b. Thing
    c. Undefined
    d. Undefined

112. A _____ is the result of the addition of a set of numbers. The numbers may be natural numbers, complex numbers, matrices, or still more complicated objects. An infinite _____ is a subtle procedure known as a series.
    a. Sum0
    b. Thing
    c. Undefined
    d. Undefined

Chapter 4. Nonlinear Functions and Equations

113. In geometry, a _____ (Greek words diairo = divide and metro = measure) of a circle is any straight line segment that passes through the centre and whose endpoints are on the circular boundary, or, in more modern usage, the length of such a line segment. When using the word in the more modern sense, one speaks of the _____ rather than a _____, because all diameters of a circle have the same length. This length is twice the radius. The _____ of a circle is also the longest chord that the circle has.
   a. Thing
   b. Diameter0
   c. Undefined
   d. Undefined

114. In mathematics, a _____ is the set of all points in three-dimensional space (R^3) which are at distance r from a fixed point of that space, where r is a positive real number called the radius of the _____. The fixed point is called the center or centre, and is not part of the _____ itself.
   a. Sphere0
   b. Thing
   c. Undefined
   d. Undefined

115. _____ is mass m per unit volume V.
   a. Thing
   b. Density0
   c. Undefined
   d. Undefined

116. Acid _____ ratio measures the ability of a company to use its near cash or quick assets to immediately extinguish its current liabilities.
   a. Thing
   b. Test0
   c. Undefined
   d. Undefined

117. In mathematics, a _____ number is a number which can be expressed as a ratio of two integers. Non-integer _____ numbers (commonly called fractions) are usually written as the vulgar fraction a / b, where b is not zero.
   a. Thing
   b. Rational0
   c. Undefined
   d. Undefined

118. _____ is a fixed, but possibly unspecified, value. This is in contrast to a variable, which is not fixed.
   a. Constant term0
   b. Thing
   c. Undefined
   d. Undefined

119. In mathematics, a _____ is a polynomial equation of the second degree. The general form is $ax^2 + bx + c = 0$.
   a. Thing
   b. Quadratic equation0
   c. Undefined
   d. Undefined

120. In mathematics, a _____ is a polynomial equation of the third degree.
   a. Cubic equation0
   b. Thing
   c. Undefined
   d. Undefined

121. In abstract algebra, _____ consists of sets with binary operations that satisfy certain axioms.
   a. Thing
   b. Grouping0
   c. Undefined
   d. Undefined

122. A _____ is a unit of length in the metric system, equal to one thousand metres, the current SI base unit of length

Chapter 4. Nonlinear Functions and Equations

a. Kilometer0
b. Thing
c. Undefined
d. Undefined

123. In mathematics, an _____ number is a complex number whose square is a negative real number. They were defined in 1572 by Rafael Bombelli.
   a. Thing
   b. Imaginary0
   c. Undefined
   d. Undefined

124. A _____ is a symbol or group of symbols, or a word in a natural language that represents a number.
   a. Thing
   b. Numeral0
   c. Undefined
   d. Undefined

125. _____ numerals are a numeral system originating in ancient Rome, adapted from Etruscan numerals.
   a. Thing
   b. Roman0
   c. Undefined
   d. Undefined

126. In mathematics, the _____ i (or sometimes the Latin j or the Greek iota, see below) allows the real number system R to be extended to the complex number system C. Its precise definition is dependent upon the particular method of extension.
   a. Thing
   b. Imaginary unit0
   c. Undefined
   d. Undefined

127. In mathematics, a _____ is a number in the form of a + bi where a and b are real numbers, and i is the imaginary unit, with the property i 2 = −1. The real number a is called the real part of the _____, and the real number b is the imaginary part.
   a. Complex number0
   b. Thing
   c. Undefined
   d. Undefined

128. _____ is a notation for writing numbers that is often used by scientists and mathematicians to make it easier to write large and small numbers.
   a. Scientific notation0
   b. Thing
   c. Undefined
   d. Undefined

129. In mathematics, an _____ is a complex number whose square is a negative real number. They were defined in 1572 by Rafael Bombelli.
   a. Thing
   b. Imaginary number0
   c. Undefined
   d. Undefined

130. In plane geometry, a _____ is a polygon with four equal sides, four right angles, and parallel opposite sides. In algebra, the _____ of a number is that number multiplied by itself.
   a. Thing
   b. Square0
   c. Undefined
   d. Undefined

131. In mathematics, a _____ of a number x is a number r such that $r^2 = x$, or in words, a number r whose square (the result of multiplying the number by itself) is x.

a. Thing
b. Square root0
c. Undefined
d. Undefined

132. _____ or arithmetics is the oldest and most elementary branch of mathematics, used by almost everyone, for tasks ranging from simple daily counting to advanced science and business calculations.
   a. Arithmetic0
   b. Thing
   c. Undefined
   d. Undefined

133. The traditional _____ are addition, subtraction, multiplication and division, although more advanced operations (such as manipulations of percentages, square root, exponentiation, and logarithmic functions) are also sometimes included in this subject.
   a. Concept
   b. Arithmetic operations0
   c. Undefined
   d. Undefined

134. In mathematics, the _____ of a complex number z, is the second element of the ordered pair of real numbers representing z, i.e. if z = (x,y), or equivalently, z = x + iy, then the _____ of z is y.
   a. Imaginary part0
   b. Thing
   c. Undefined
   d. Undefined

135. In algebra, a _____ is a binomial formed by taking the opposite of the second term of a binomial.
   a. Thing
   b. Conjugate0
   c. Undefined
   d. Undefined

136. _____ of a polynomial with real or complex coefficients is a certain expression in the coefficients of the polynomial which is equal to zero if and only if the polynomial has a multiple root i.e. a root with multiplicity greater than one in the complex numbers.
   a. Thing
   b. Discriminant0
   c. Undefined
   d. Undefined

137. In number theory, the _____ of arithmetic (or unique factorization theorem) states that every natural number greater than 1 can be written as a unique product of prime numbers.
   a. Fundamental theorem0
   b. Concept
   c. Undefined
   d. Undefined

138. _____ states that every non-zero single-variable polynomial, with complex coefficients, has exactly as many complex roots as its degree, if repeated roots are counted up to their multiplicity.
   a. Fundamental theorem of algebra0
   b. Thing
   c. Undefined
   d. Undefined

139. The _____ of an algebraic expression is the same equation, but without parentheses.
   a. Expanded form0
   b. Thing
   c. Undefined
   d. Undefined

140. The _____ is the maximum of the degrees of all terms in the polynomial.

Chapter 4. Nonlinear Functions and Equations

    a. Thing
    b. Degree of a polynomial0
    c. Undefined
    d. Undefined

141. _____ is the difference of electrical potential between two points of an electrical or electronic circuit, expressed in volts
    a. Thing
    b. Voltage0
    c. Undefined
    d. Undefined

142. Electrical _____, or simply _____, is a term coined by Oliver Heaviside in July of 1886 to describe a measure of opposition to a sinusoidal alternating current.
    a. Thing
    b. Impedance0
    c. Undefined
    d. Undefined

143. In mathematics, _____ expressions is used to reduce the expression into the lowest possible term.
    a. Thing
    b. Simplifying0
    c. Undefined
    d. Undefined

144. In mathematics, a _____ is any function which can be written as the ratio of two polynomial functions.
    a. Thing
    b. Rational function0
    c. Undefined
    d. Undefined

145. In mathematics, a _____ is a number which can be expressed as a ratio of two integers. Non-integer rational numbers (commonly called fractions) are usually written as the vulgar fraction a / b, where b is not zero.
    a. Concept
    b. Rational Number0
    c. Undefined
    d. Undefined

146. An _____ is a straight line or curve A to which another curve B approaches closer and closer as one moves along it. As one moves along B, the space between it and the _____ A becomes smaller and smaller, and can in fact be made as small as one could wish by going far enough along. A curve may or may not touch or cross its _____. In fact, the curve may intersect the _____ an infinite number of times.
    a. Asymptote0
    b. Thing
    c. Undefined
    d. Undefined

147. A _____ is the part of a fraction that tells how many equal parts make up a whole, and which is used in the name of the fraction: "halves", "thirds", "fourths" or "quarters", "fifths" and so on.
    a. Denominator0
    b. Concept
    c. Undefined
    d. Undefined

148. _____ is a straight line or curve A to which another curve B the one being studied approaches closer and closer as one moves along it.
    a. Thing
    b. Vertical asymptote0
    c. Undefined
    d. Undefined

149. In mathematics, defined and _____ are used to explain whether or not expressions have meaningful, sensible, and unambiguous values.

a. Thing
b. Undefined0
c. Undefined
d. Undefined

150. _____ is the chance that something is likely to happen or be the case.
   a. Thing
   b. Probability0
   c. Undefined
   d. Undefined

151. In mathematics, a _____ in elementary terms is any of a variety of different functions from geometry, such as rotations, reflections and translations.
   a. Thing
   b. Transformation0
   c. Undefined
   d. Undefined

152. The _____ of measurement are a globally standardized and modernized form of the metric system.
   a. Thing
   b. Units0
   c. Undefined
   d. Undefined

153. In mathematics, a _____ (also spelled reflexion) is a map that transforms an object into its mirror image.
   a. Reflection0
   b. Concept
   c. Undefined
   d. Undefined

154. _____ is the largest positive integer that divides both numbers without remainder.
   a. Common Factor0
   b. Thing
   c. Undefined
   d. Undefined

155. In statistics, _____ means the most frequent value assumed by a random variable, or occurring in a sampling of a random variable.
   a. Mode0
   b. Concept
   c. Undefined
   d. Undefined

156. _____ are external two-dimensional outlines, with the appearance or configuration of some thing - in contrast to the matter or content or substance of which it is composed.
   a. Shapes0
   b. Thing
   c. Undefined
   d. Undefined

157. In mathematics and logic, a _____ proof is a way of showing the truth or falsehood of a given statement by a straightforward combination of established facts, usually existing lemmas and theorems, without making any further assumptions.
   a. Direct0
   b. Thing
   c. Undefined
   d. Undefined

158. _____ is the relationship between two variables, like a ratio in which the two quantities being compared are different units.
   a. Direct variation0
   b. Thing
   c. Undefined
   d. Undefined

159. A _____ is an object that is attached to a pivot point so that it can swing freely.

Chapter 4. Nonlinear Functions and Equations

    a. Thing
    c. Undefined
    b. Pendulum0
    d. Undefined

160. In mathematics, two quantities are called _____ if they vary in such a way that one of the quantities is a constant multiple of the other, or equivalently if they have a constant ratio.
    a. Thing
    c. Undefined
    b. Proportional0
    d. Undefined

161. _____ is the transport of people on a trip/journey or the process or time involved in a person or object moving from one location to another.
    a. Thing
    c. Undefined
    b. Travel0
    d. Undefined

162. _____ element of an element x with respect to a binary operation * with identity element e is an element y such that x * y = y * x = e. In particular,
    a. Thing
    c. Undefined
    b. Inverse0
    d. Undefined

163. _____ is electromagnetic radiation with a wavelength that is visible to the eye (visible _____) or, in a technical or scientific context, electromagnetic radiation of any wavelength.
    a. Thing
    c. Undefined
    b. Light0
    d. Undefined

164. The metre (or _____, see spelling differences) is a measure of length. It is the basic unit of length in the metric system and in the International System of Units (SI), used around the world for general and scientific purposes.
    a. Concept
    c. Undefined
    b. Meter0
    d. Undefined

165. Initial objects are also called _____, and terminal objects are also called final.
    a. Thing
    c. Undefined
    b. Coterminal0
    d. Undefined

166. _____ Any process by which a specified characteristic usually amplitude of the output of a device is prevented from exceeding a predetermined value.
    a. Thing
    c. Undefined
    b. Limiting0
    d. Undefined

167. In mathematics, a _____ is a quadric surface, with the following equation in Cartesian coordinates: $(x/a)^2 + (y/b)^2 = 1$.
    a. Cylinder0
    c. Undefined
    b. Thing
    d. Undefined

168. Compass and straightedge or ruler-and-compass _____ is the _____ of lengths or angles using only an idealized ruler and compass.

Chapter 4. Nonlinear Functions and Equations

a. Construction0
b. Thing
c. Undefined
d. Undefined

169. _____ is a way of expressing a number as a fraction of 100 per cent meaning "per hundred".
a. Percent0
b. Thing
c. Undefined
d. Undefined

170. The _____ of a geographic location is its height above a fixed reference point, often the mean sea level.
a. Elevation0
b. Thing
c. Undefined
d. Undefined

171. A _____ is a function that assigns a number to subsets of a given set.
a. Measure0
b. Thing
c. Undefined
d. Undefined

172. _____ is a special mathematical relationship between two quantities. Two quantities are called proportional if they vary in such a way that one of the quantities is a constant multiple of the other, or equivalently if they have a constant ratio.
a. Thing
b. Proportionality0
c. Undefined
d. Undefined

173. In classical geometry, a _____ of a circle or sphere is any line segment from its center to its boundary. By extension, the _____ of a circle or sphere is the length of any such segment. The _____ is half the diameter. In science and engineering the term _____ of curvature is commonly used as a synonym for _____.
a. Thing
b. Radius0
c. Undefined
d. Undefined

174. In _____ algebra, a *-ring is an associative ring with an antilinear, antiautomorphism * : A ¨ A which is an involution.
a. Star0
b. Thing
c. Undefined
d. Undefined

175. _____ is a set, with some particular properties and usually some additional structure, such as the operations of addition or multiplication, for instance.
a. Space0
b. Thing
c. Undefined
d. Undefined

176. In geometry, a _____ is the intersection of a body in 2-dimensional space with a line, or of a body in 3-dimensional space with a plane
a. Cross section0
b. Thing
c. Undefined
d. Undefined

177. _____ is a reaction force applied by a stretched string on the objects which stretch it.
a. Tension0
b. Thing
c. Undefined
d. Undefined

Chapter 4. Nonlinear Functions and Equations

178. In statistics the _____ of an event i is the number n_i of times the event occurred in the experiment or the study. These frequencies are often graphically represented in histograms.
- a. Concept
- b. Frequency0
- c. Undefined
- d. Undefined

179. In mathematics, an _____ is a statement about the relative size or order of two objects.
- a. Inequality0
- b. Thing
- c. Undefined
- d. Undefined

180. A _____ is a set of possible values that a variable can take on in order to satisfy a given set of conditions, which may include equations and inequalities.
- a. Solution set0
- b. Thing
- c. Undefined
- d. Undefined

181. In mathematics, two sets are said to be _____ if they have no element in common. For example, {1, 2, 3} and {4, 5, 6} are sets which are _____.
- a. Disjoint0
- b. Thing
- c. Undefined
- d. Undefined

182. _____ is the force that opposes the relative motion or tendency toward such motion of two surfaces in contact.
- a. Thing
- b. Friction0
- c. Undefined
- d. Undefined

183. In physics, an _____ is the path that an object makes around another object while under the influence of a source of centripetal force, such as gravity.
- a. Orbit0
- b. Thing
- c. Undefined
- d. Undefined

184. A _____, as defined by the International Astronomical Union , is a celestial body orbiting a star or stellar remnant that is massive enough to be rounded by its own gravity, not massive enough to cause thermonuclear fusion in its core, and has cleared its neighboring region of planetesimals.
- a. Thing
- b. Planet0
- c. Undefined
- d. Undefined

185. _____ is a mathematical operation, written a^n, involving two numbers, the base a and the exponent n.
- a. Thing
- b. Exponentiating0
- c. Undefined
- d. Undefined

186. _____ is a mathematical operation, written a^n, involving two numbers, the base a and the exponent n.
- a. Exponentiation0
- b. Thing
- c. Undefined
- d. Undefined

187. The _____ or kilogramme is the SI base unit of mass. It is defined as being equal to the mass of the international prototype of the _____.

Chapter 4. Nonlinear Functions and Equations

a. Thing
b. Kilogram0
c. Undefined
d. Undefined

188. _____, either of the curved-bracket punctuation marks that together make a set of _____
a. Thing
b. Parentheses0
c. Undefined
d. Undefined

189. The function difference divided by the point difference is known as the _____
a. Difference quotient0
b. Thing
c. Undefined
d. Undefined

190. _____ is a free computer algebra system based on a 1982 version of Macsyma
a. Maxima0
b. Thing
c. Undefined
d. Undefined

191. _____ is a term applied when talking about the movement of air from one place to the next.
a. Thing
b. Wind speed0
c. Undefined
d. Undefined

192. Sir Isaac _____, was an English physicist, mathematician, astronomer, natural philosopher, and alchemist, regarded by many as the greatest figure in the history of science
a. Person
b. Newton0
c. Undefined
d. Undefined

193. In mathematics, the _____ of a function is the set of all "output" values produced by that function. Given a function $f : A \to B$, the _____ of f, is defined to be the set $\{x \in B : x = f(a) \text{ for some } a \in A\}$.
a. Range0
b. Thing
c. Undefined
d. Undefined

194. _____ is often used to describe the measurement of the steepness, incline, gradient, or grade of a straight line. The _____ is defined as the ratio of the "rise" divided by the "run" between two points on a line, or in other words, the ratio of the altitude change to the horizontal distance between any two points on the line.
a. Slope0
b. Thing
c. Undefined
d. Undefined

195. In geometry, two lines or planes if one falls on the other in such a way as to create congruent adjacent angles. The term may be used as a noun or adjective. Thus, referring to Figure 1, the line AB is the _____ to CD through the point B.
a. Thing
b. Perpendicular0
c. Undefined
d. Undefined

196. _____ is a technique used in algebra to solve quadratic equations, in analytic geometry for determining the shapes of graphs, and in calculus for computing integrals, including, but hardly limited to, the integrals that define Laplace transforms. The essential objective is to reduce a quadratic polynomial in a variable in an equation or expression to a squared polynomial of linear order. This can reduce an equation or integral to one that is more easily solved or evaluated.

Chapter 4. Nonlinear Functions and Equations

    a. Thing
    c. Undefined
    b. Completing the square0
    d. Undefined

197. A _____ is a three-dimensional geometric shape formed by straight lines through a fixed point (vertex) to the points of a fixed curve (directrix)
    a. Cone0
    c. Undefined
    b. Concept
    d. Undefined

198. In Euclidean geometry, an _____ is a closed segment of a differentiable curve in the two-dimensional plane; for example, a circular _____ is a segment of a circle.
    a. Concept
    c. Undefined
    b. Arc0
    d. Undefined

199. _____ is the level of functional and/or metabolic efficiency of an organism at both the micro level.
    a. Thing
    c. Undefined
    b. Health0
    d. Undefined

200. The population _____ is the total number of human beings alive on the planet Earth at a given time.
    a. Thing
    c. Undefined
    b. Of the world0
    d. Undefined

201. The _____ is the total number of human beings alive on the planet Earth at a given time.
    a. Thing
    c. Undefined
    b. World population0
    d. Undefined

202. In mathematics, a _____ of a number x is the exponent y of the power by such that $x = b^y$. The value used for the base b must be neither 0 nor 1, nor a root of 1 in the case of the extension to complex numbers, and is typically 10, e, or 2.
    a. Thing
    c. Undefined
    b. Logarithm0
    d. Undefined

203. A _____ is a deliberate process for transforming one or more inputs into one or more results.
    a. Calculation0
    c. Undefined
    b. Thing
    d. Undefined

Chapter 5. Exponential and Logarithmic Functions

1. In mathematics, _____ is an elementary arithmetic operation. When one of the numbers is a whole number, _____ is the repeated sum of the other number.
   - a. Thing
   - b. Multiplication0
   - c. Undefined
   - d. Undefined

2. A _____ is a symbolic representation denoting a quantity or expression. It often represents an "unknown" quantity that has the potential to change.
   - a. Variable0
   - b. Thing
   - c. Undefined
   - d. Undefined

3. The mathematical concept of a _____ expresses the intuitive idea of deterministic dependence between two quantities, one of which is viewed as primary and the other as secondary. A _____ then is a way to associate a unique output for each input of a specified type, for example, a real number or an element of a given set.
   - a. Thing
   - b. Function0
   - c. Undefined
   - d. Undefined

4. _____ or arithmetics is the oldest and most elementary branch of mathematics, used by almost everyone, for tasks ranging from simple daily counting to advanced science and business calculations.
   - a. Arithmetic0
   - b. Thing
   - c. Undefined
   - d. Undefined

5. The traditional _____ are addition, subtraction, multiplication and division, although more advanced operations (such as manipulations of percentages, square root, exponentiation, and logarithmic functions) are also sometimes included in this subject.
   - a. Concept
   - b. Arithmetic operations0
   - c. Undefined
   - d. Undefined

6. A _____ is the result of the addition of a set of numbers. The numbers may be natural numbers, complex numbers, matrices, or still more complicated objects. An infinite _____ is a subtle procedure known as a series.
   - a. Thing
   - b. Sum0
   - c. Undefined
   - d. Undefined

7. _____ is the transport of people on a trip/journey or the process or time involved in a person or object moving from one location to another.
   - a. Thing
   - b. Travel0
   - c. Undefined
   - d. Undefined

8. In mathematics and the mathematical sciences, a _____ is a fixed, but possibly unspecified, value. This is in contrast to a variable, which is not fixed.
   - a. Constant0
   - b. Thing
   - c. Undefined
   - d. Undefined

9. A _____ is a unit of length, usually used to measure distance, in a number of different systems, including Imperial units, United States customary units and Norwegian/Swedish mil. Its size can vary from system to system, but in each is between 1 and 10 kilometers. In contemporary English contexts _____ refers to either:

Chapter 5. Exponential and Logarithmic Functions

  a. Thing
  c. Undefined
  b. Mile0
  d. Undefined

10. _____ is a unit of speed, expressing the number of international miles covered per hour.
  a. Thing
  c. Undefined
  b. Miles per hour0
  d. Undefined

11. In mathematics, a _____ of a k-place relation $L \subseteq X_1 \times \ldots \times X_k$ is one of the sets X_j, $1 \le j \le k$. In the special case where k = 2 and $L \subseteq X_1 \times X_2$ is a function $L : X_1 \to X_2$, it is conventional to refer to X_1 as the _____ of the function and to refer to X_2 as the codomain of the function.
  a. Domain0
  c. Undefined
  b. Thing
  d. Undefined

12. An _____ is a combination of numbers, operators, grouping symbols and/or free variables and bound variables arranged in a meaningful way which can be evaluated..
  a. Expression0
  c. Undefined
  b. Thing
  d. Undefined

13. In mathematics, a _____ is the result of multiplying, or an expression that identifies factors to be multiplied.
  a. Thing
  c. Undefined
  b. Product0
  d. Undefined

14. In mathematics, defined and _____ are used to explain whether or not expressions have meaningful, sensible, and unambiguous values.
  a. Thing
  c. Undefined
  b. Undefined0
  d. Undefined

15. In mathematics, a _____ is the end result of a division problem. It can also be expressed as the number of times the divisor divides into the dividend.
  a. Thing
  c. Undefined
  b. Quotient0
  d. Undefined

16. In mathematics, the _____ of a coordinate system is the point where the axes of the system intersect.
  a. Thing
  c. Undefined
  b. Origin0
  d. Undefined

17. A _____ is a deliberate process for transforming one or more inputs into one or more results.
  a. Calculation0
  c. Undefined
  b. Thing
  d. Undefined

18. In mathematics, a subset of Euclidean space R^n is called _____ if it is closed and bounded.
  a. Compact0
  c. Undefined
  b. Thing
  d. Undefined

Chapter 5. Exponential and Logarithmic Functions

19. _____, from Latin meaning "to make progress", is defined in two different ways. Pure economic _____ is the increase in wealth that an investor has from making an investment, taking into consideration all costs associated with that investment including the opportunity cost of capital.
    a. Thing
    b. Profit0
    c. Undefined
    d. Undefined

20. Fixed costs are expenses whose total does not change in proportion to the activity of a business.Unit fixed costs decline with volume following a retangular hyperbola as the volume of production.Variable costs by contrast change in relation to the activity of a business such as sales or production volume.Along with variable costs,fixed costs make up one of the two components of total cost. In the most simple production function total cost is equal to fixed costs plus variable costs.In accounting terminology, fixed costs will broadly include all costs which are not included in cost of goods sold, and variable costs are those captured in costs of goods sold. The implicit assumption required to make the equivalence between the accounting and economics terminology is that the accounting period is equal to the period in which fixed costs do not vary in relation to production. In practice, this equivalence does not always hold and depending on the period under consideration by management, some overhead expenses can be adjusted by management, and the specific allocation of each expense to each category will be decided under cost accounting.In business planning and management accounting, usage of the terms fixed costs, variable costs and others will often differ from usage in economics, and may depend on the intended use. For example, costs may be segregated into per unit costs fixed costs per period, and variable costs as a proportion of revenue. Capital expenditures will usually be allocated separately, and depending on the purpose, a portion may be regularly allocated to expenses as depreciation and amortization and seen as a _____ per period, or the entire amount may be considered upfront fixed costs.
    a. Thing
    b. Fixed cost0
    c. Undefined
    d. Undefined

21. _____ is the application of tools and a processing medium to the transformation of raw materials into finished goods for sale.
    a. Thing
    b. Manufacturing0
    c. Undefined
    d. Undefined

22. _____ is a business term for the amount of money that a company receives from its activities in a given period, mostly from sales of products and/or services to customers
    a. Thing
    b. Revenue0
    c. Undefined
    d. Undefined

23. The plus and _____ signs are mathematical symbols used to represent the notions of positive and negative as well as the operations of addition and subtraction.
    a. Minus0
    b. Thing
    c. Undefined
    d. Undefined

24. Mathematical _____ is used to represent ideas.
    a. Thing
    b. Notation0
    c. Undefined
    d. Undefined

25. In mathematics, a _____ is an ordered list of objects. Like a set, it contains members, also called elements or terms, and the number of terms is called the length of the _____. Unlike a set, order matters, and the exact same elements can appear multiple times at different positions in the _____.

Chapter 5. Exponential and Logarithmic Functions

    a. Thing
    b. Sequence0
    c. Undefined
    d. Undefined

26. In mathematics, a _____ of a positive integer n is a way of writing n as a sum of positive integers.
    a. Thing
    b. Composition0
    c. Undefined
    d. Undefined

27. Equivalence is the condition of being _____ or essentially equal.
    a. Thing
    b. Equivalent0
    c. Undefined
    d. Undefined

28. The _____ functions is determined by the nesting of two or more functions to form a single new function.
    a. Composition of two0
    b. Thing
    c. Undefined
    d. Undefined

29. A _____ number is a positive integer which has a positive divisor other than one or itself.
    a. Thing
    b. Composite0
    c. Undefined
    d. Undefined

30. A _____, formed by the composition of one function on another, represents the application of the former to the result of the application of the latter to the argument of the composite.
    a. Thing
    b. Composite function0
    c. Undefined
    d. Undefined

31. Mathematical _____ are the wide variety of ways to capture an abstract mathematical concept or relationship.
    a. Thing
    b. Representations0
    c. Undefined
    d. Undefined

32. In mathematics, a _____ may be described informally as a number that can be given by an infinite decimal representation.
    a. Thing
    b. Real number0
    c. Undefined
    d. Undefined

33. _____ are the basic objects of study in graph theory. Informally speaking, a graph is a set of objects called points, nodes, or vertices connected by links called lines or edges.
    a. Graphs0
    b. Thing
    c. Undefined
    d. Undefined

34. _____ is a kind of property which exists as magnitude or multitude. It is among the basic classes of things along with quality, substance, change, and relation.
    a. Amount0
    b. Thing
    c. Undefined
    d. Undefined

35. The _____, the average in everyday English, which is also called the arithmetic _____ (and is distinguished from the geometric _____ or harmonic _____). The average is also called the sample _____. The expected value of a random variable, which is also called the population _____.

Chapter 5. Exponential and Logarithmic Functions

    a. Mean0
    c. Undefined
    b. Thing
    d. Undefined

36. In mathematics, an _____, mean, or central tendency of a data set refers to a measure of the "middle" or "expected" value of the data set.
    a. Average0
    c. Undefined
    b. Concept
    d. Undefined

37. _____ is, or relates to, the _____ temperature scale .
    a. Celsius0
    c. Undefined
    b. Thing
    d. Undefined

38. In mathematics, there are several meanings of _____ depending on the subject.
    a. Degree0
    c. Undefined
    b. Thing
    d. Undefined

39. _____ is a physical property of a system that underlies the common notions of hot and cold; something that is hotter has the greater _____.
    a. Temperature0
    c. Undefined
    b. Thing
    d. Undefined

40. _____ is a way of expressing a number as a fraction of 100 per cent meaning "per hundred".
    a. Thing
    c. Undefined
    b. Percent0
    d. Undefined

41. In economics, supply and _____ describe market relations between prospective sellers and buyers of a good.
    a. Thing
    c. Undefined
    b. Demand0
    d. Undefined

42. In geometry, a _____ is defined as a quadrilateral where all four of its angles are right angles.
    a. Rectangle0
    c. Undefined
    b. Thing
    d. Undefined

43. Multiple Signal Classification, also known as _____, is an algorithm used for frequency estimation and emitter location.
    a. Music0
    c. Undefined
    b. Thing
    d. Undefined

44. U.S. liquid _____ is legally defined as 231 cubic inches, and is equal to 3.785411784 litres or abotu 0.13368 cubic feet. This is the most common definition of a _____. The U.S. fluid ounce is defined as 1/128 of a U.S. _____.
    a. Gallon0
    c. Undefined
    b. Thing
    d. Undefined

45. The word _____ comes from the Latin word linearis, which means created by lines.

Chapter 5. Exponential and Logarithmic Functions

    a. Thing
    b. Linear0
    c. Undefined
    d. Undefined

46. In mathematics, a matrix can be thought of as each row or _____ being a vector. Hence, a space formed by row vectors or _____ vectors are said to be a row space or a _____ space.
    a. Concept
    b. Column0
    c. Undefined
    d. Undefined

47. _____ is a temperature scale named after the German physicist Daniel Gabriel _____ , who proposed it in 1724.
    a. Thing
    b. Fahrenheit0
    c. Undefined
    d. Undefined

48. _____ of an object is its speed in a particular direction.
    a. Velocity0
    b. Thing
    c. Undefined
    d. Undefined

49. The _____ of an object is the extra energy which it possesses due to its motion.
    a. Thing
    b. Kinetic energy0
    c. Undefined
    d. Undefined

50. In physics, a _____ may refer to the scalar _____ or to the vector _____ .
    a. Potential0
    b. Thing
    c. Undefined
    d. Undefined

51. In classical geometry, a _____ of a circle or sphere is any line segment from its center to its boundary. By extension, the _____ of a circle or sphere is the length of any such segment. The _____ is half the diameter. In science and engineering the term _____ of curvature is commonly used as a synonym for _____ .
    a. Thing
    b. Radius0
    c. Undefined
    d. Undefined

52. A _____ is a special kind of ratio, indicating a relationship between two measurements with different units, such as miles to gallons or cents to pounds.
    a. Rate0
    b. Thing
    c. Undefined
    d. Undefined

53. In plane geometry, a _____ is a polygon with four equal sides, four right angles, and parallel opposite sides. In algebra, the _____ of a number is that number multiplied by itself.
    a. Thing
    b. Square0
    c. Undefined
    d. Undefined

54. The _____ of measurement are a globally standardized and modernized form of the metric system.
    a. Thing
    b. Units0
    c. Undefined
    d. Undefined

55. In mathematics a _____ is a function which defines a distance between elements of a set.

Chapter 5. Exponential and Logarithmic Functions

a. Metric0
b. Thing
c. Undefined
d. Undefined

56. A _____ is a quantity that denotes the proportional amount or magnitude of one quantity relative to another.
   a. Thing
   b. Ratio0
   c. Undefined
   d. Undefined

57. In Euclidean geometry, an _____ is a closed segment of a differentiable curve in the two-dimensional plane; for example, a circular _____ is a segment of a circle.
   a. Concept
   b. Arc0
   c. Undefined
   d. Undefined

58. A _____ is one of the basic shapes of geometry: a polygon with three vertices and three sides which are straight line segments.
   a. Thing
   b. Triangle0
   c. Undefined
   d. Undefined

59. In geometry, an _____ polygon is a polygon which has all sides of the same length.
   a. Equilateral0
   b. Thing
   c. Undefined
   d. Undefined

60. An _____ is a triangle in which all sides are of equal length.
   a. Thing
   b. Equilateral triangle0
   c. Undefined
   d. Undefined

61. A _____ is a first degree polynomial mathematical function of the form: f(x) = mx + b where m and b are real constants and x is a real variable.
   a. Linear function0
   b. Thing
   c. Undefined
   d. Undefined

62. _____ is a function whose values do not vary and thus are constant.
   a. Thing
   b. Constant function0
   c. Undefined
   d. Undefined

63. _____ element of an element x with respect to a binary operation * with identity element e is an element y such that x * y = y * x = e. In particular,
   a. Inverse0
   b. Thing
   c. Undefined
   d. Undefined

64. An _____ is a function which does the reverse of a given function.
   a. Thing
   b. Inverse function0
   c. Undefined
   d. Undefined

65. A _____ are accounts maintained by commercial banks, savings and loan associations, credit unions, and mutual savings banks that pay interest but can not be used directly as money by, for example, writing a cheque.

Chapter 5. Exponential and Logarithmic Functions

    a. Thing
    c. Undefined
    b. Savings account0
    d. Undefined

66. In mathematical logic, a Gödel numbering (or Gödel _____) is a function that assigns to each symbol and well-formed formula of some formal language a unique natural number called its Gödel number.
    a. Thing
    c. Undefined
    b. Code0
    d. Undefined

67. _____ is a mathematical operation, written a^n, involving two numbers, the base a and the exponent n.
    a. Exponentiating0
    c. Undefined
    b. Thing
    d. Undefined

68. _____ is a mathematical operation, written a^n, involving two numbers, the base a and the exponent n.
    a. Thing
    c. Undefined
    b. Exponentiation0
    d. Undefined

69. An _____ or member of a set is an object that when collected together make up the set.
    a. Element0
    c. Undefined
    b. Thing
    d. Undefined

70. In mathematics, the _____ , or members of a set or more generally a class are all those objects which when collected together make up the set or class.
    a. Thing
    c. Undefined
    b. Elements0
    d. Undefined

71. In astronomy, geography, geometry and related sciences and contexts, a plane is said to be _____ at a given point if it is locally perpendicular to the gradient of the gravity field, i.e., with the direction of the gravitational force at that point.
    a. Horizontal0
    c. Undefined
    b. Thing
    d. Undefined

72. _____ the expected value of a random variable displays the average or central value of the variable. It is a summary value of the distribution of the variable.
    a. Determining0
    c. Undefined
    b. Thing
    d. Undefined

73. _____ is a test used to determine if a function is injective, surjective or bijective.
    a. Thing
    c. Undefined
    b. Horizontal line test0
    d. Undefined

74. Acid _____ ratio measures the ability of a company to use its near cash or quick assets to immediately extinguish its current liabilities.
    a. Test0
    c. Undefined
    b. Thing
    d. Undefined

75. In mathematics, the _____ of a function is the set of all "output" values produced by that function. Given a function $f : A \to B$, the _____ of f, is defined to be the set $\{x \in B : x = f(a) \text{ for some } a \in A\}$.

Chapter 5. Exponential and Logarithmic Functions 85

    a. Thing
    b. Range0
    c. Undefined
    d. Undefined

76. A _____ is a three-dimensional solid object bounded by six square faces, facets, or sides, with three meeting at each vertex.
    a. Cube0
    b. Thing
    c. Undefined
    d. Undefined

77. A _____ of a number is a number a such that $a^3 = x$.
    a. Thing
    b. Cube root0
    c. Undefined
    d. Undefined

78. _____ are of a number n in its third power-the result of multiplying it by itself three times.
    a. Cubes0
    b. Thing
    c. Undefined
    d. Undefined

79. In mathematics, a _____ of a complex-valued function f is a member x of the domain of f such that f(x) vanishes at x, that is, x : f (x) = 0.
    a. Thing
    b. Root0
    c. Undefined
    d. Undefined

80. _____ is the symbol used to indicate the nth root of a number
    a. Thing
    b. Radical0
    c. Undefined
    d. Undefined

81. In mathematics, a _____ number is a number which can be expressed as a ratio of two integers. Non-integer _____ numbers (commonly called fractions) are usually written as the vulgar fraction a / b, where b is not zero.
    a. Rational0
    b. Thing
    c. Undefined
    d. Undefined

82. _____ is often used to describe the measurement of the steepness, incline, gradient, or grade of a straight line. The _____ is defined as the ratio of the "rise" divided by the "run" between two points on a line, or in other words, the ratio of the altitude change to the horizontal distance between any two points on the line.
    a. Thing
    b. Slope0
    c. Undefined
    d. Undefined

83. A _____ is a simplified and structured visual representation of concepts, ideas, constructions, relations, statistical data, anatomy etc used in all aspects of human activities to visualize and clarify the topic.
    a. Diagram0
    b. Thing
    c. Undefined
    d. Undefined

84. In geometry, a line _____ is a part of a line that is bounded by two end points, and contains every point on the line between its end points.
    a. Concept
    b. Segment0
    c. Undefined
    d. Undefined

Chapter 5. Exponential and Logarithmic Functions

85. A _____ is a part of a line that is bounded by two end points, and contains every point on the line between its end points.
   a. Thing
   b. Line segment0
   c. Undefined
   d. Undefined

86. In geometry, two lines or planes if one falls on the other in such a way as to create congruent adjacent angles. The term may be used as a noun or adjective. Thus, referring to Figure 1, the line AB is the _____ to CD through the point B.
   a. Perpendicular0
   b. Thing
   c. Undefined
   d. Undefined

87. In mathematics, a _____ (also spelled reflexion) is a map that transforms an object into its mirror image.
   a. Concept
   b. Reflection0
   c. Undefined
   d. Undefined

88. In mathematics, _____ is a part of the set theoretic notion of function.
   a. Thing
   b. Image0
   c. Undefined
   d. Undefined

89. The _____ of an angle is the ratio of the length of the adjacent side to the length of the hypotenuse.
   a. Concept
   b. Cosine0
   c. Undefined
   d. Undefined

90. In common philosophical language, a proposition or _____, is the content of an assertion, that is, it is true-or-false and defined by the meaning of a particular piece of language.
   a. Statement0
   b. Concept
   c. Undefined
   d. Undefined

91. _____ is electromagnetic radiation with a wavelength that is visible to the eye (visible _____) or, in a technical or scientific context, electromagnetic radiation of any wavelength.
   a. Thing
   b. Light0
   c. Undefined
   d. Undefined

92. In mathematics, the multiplicative inverse of a number x, denoted 1/x or x^{-1}, is the number which, when multiplied by x, yields 1. The multiplicative inverse of x is also called the _____ of x.
   a. Thing
   b. Reciprocal0
   c. Undefined
   d. Undefined

93. _____ are a measure of time.
   a. Thing
   b. Minutes0
   c. Undefined
   d. Undefined

94. The _____ of a solid object is the three-dimensional concept of how much space it occupies, often quantified numerically.
   a. Volume0
   b. Thing
   c. Undefined
   d. Undefined

Chapter 5. Exponential and Logarithmic Functions

95. In mathematics, a _____ is the set of all points in three-dimensional space (R^3) which are at distance r from a fixed point of that space, where r is a positive real number called the radius of the _____. The fixed point is called the center or centre, and is not part of the _____ itself.
    a. Sphere0
    b. Thing
    c. Undefined
    d. Undefined

96. In physics, an _____ is the path that an object makes around another object while under the influence of a source of centripetal force, such as gravity.
    a. Thing
    b. Orbit0
    c. Undefined
    d. Undefined

97. A _____, as defined by the International Astronomical Union , is a celestial body orbiting a star or stellar remnant that is massive enough to be rounded by its own gravity, not massive enough to cause thermonuclear fusion in its core, and has cleared its neighboring region of planetesimals.
    a. Planet0
    b. Thing
    c. Undefined
    d. Undefined

98. The conversion of units (_____) refers to conversion factors between different units of measurement for the same quantity.
    a. Concept
    b. Converting units0
    c. Undefined
    d. Undefined

99. An _____ of a product of sums expresses it as a sum of products by using the fact that multiplication distributes over addition.
    a. Thing
    b. Expansion0
    c. Undefined
    d. Undefined

100. In functional analysis and related areas of mathematics the _____ set of a given subset of a vector space is a certain set in the dual space.
    a. Polar0
    b. Thing
    c. Undefined
    d. Undefined

101. A _____ is a vehicle, missile or aircraft which obtains thrust by the reaction to the ejection of fast moving fluid from within a _____ engine.
    a. Thing
    b. Rocket0
    c. Undefined
    d. Undefined

102. _____ is the design, analysis, and/or construction of works for practical purposes.
    a. Thing
    b. Engineering0
    c. Undefined
    d. Undefined

103. In mathematics, _____ growth occurs when the growth rate of a function is always proportional to the function's current size.
    a. Thing
    b. Exponential0
    c. Undefined
    d. Undefined

104. _____ is one of the most important functions in mathematics. A function commonly used to study growth and decay
   a. Thing
   b. Exponential function0
   c. Undefined
   d. Undefined

105. _____ is the fee paid on borrowed money.
   a. Interest0
   b. Thing
   c. Undefined
   d. Undefined

106. An _____ is the fee paid on borrow money.
   a. Concept
   b. Interest rate0
   c. Undefined
   d. Undefined

107. In mathematics, _____ occurs when the growth rate of a function is always proportional to the function's current size.
   a. Exponential growth0
   b. Thing
   c. Undefined
   d. Undefined

108. In mathematics, factorization (British English: factorisation) or factoring is the decomposition of an object (for example, a number, a polynomial, or a matrix) into a product of other objects, or _____, which when multiplied together give the original.
   a. Factors0
   b. Thing
   c. Undefined
   d. Undefined

109. Initial objects are also called _____, and terminal objects are also called final.
   a. Thing
   b. Coterminal0
   c. Undefined
   d. Undefined

110. _____ has many meanings, most of which simply .
   a. Thing
   b. Power0
   c. Undefined
   d. Undefined

111. _____ is a synonym for information.
   a. Data0
   b. Thing
   c. Undefined
   d. Undefined

112. _____ means in succession or back-to-back
   a. Thing
   b. Consecutive0
   c. Undefined
   d. Undefined

113. _____ is a form of periodic payment from an employer to an employee, which is specified in an employment contract.
   a. Thing
   b. Gross pay0
   c. Undefined
   d. Undefined

Chapter 5. Exponential and Logarithmic Functions

114. A _____ is a form of periodic payment from an employer to an employee, which is specified in an employment contract.
- a. Thing
- b. Salary0
- c. Undefined
- d. Undefined

115. _____ is a decrease that follows an exponential function.
- a. Thing
- b. Exponential decay0
- c. Undefined
- d. Undefined

116. A _____ function is a function for which, intuitively, small changes in the input result in small changes in the output.
- a. Event
- b. Continuous0
- c. Undefined
- d. Undefined

117. _____ is a branch of mathematics concerning the study of structure, relation and quantity.
- a. Concept
- b. Algebra0
- c. Undefined
- d. Undefined

118. In mathematics, a _____ is an expression that is constructed from one or more variables and constants, using only the operations of addition, subtraction, multiplication, and constant positive whole number exponents. is a _____. Note in particular that division by an expression containing a variable is not in general allowed in polynomials. [1]
- a. Polynomial0
- b. Thing
- c. Undefined
- d. Undefined

119. _____ is the process in which an unstable atomic nucleus loses energy by emitting radiation in the form of particles or electromagnetic waves.
- a. Thing
- b. Radioactive decay0
- c. Undefined
- d. Undefined

120. A _____ is a function that assigns a number to subsets of a given set.
- a. Measure0
- b. Thing
- c. Undefined
- d. Undefined

121. In business, particularly accounting, a _____ is the time intervals that the accounts, statement, payments, or other calculations cover.
- a. Period0
- b. Thing
- c. Undefined
- d. Undefined

122. _____ is a subset of a population.
- a. Thing
- b. Sample0
- c. Undefined
- d. Undefined

123. In mathematics, an inequality is a statement about the relative size or order of two objects. For example 14 > 10, or 14 is _____ 10.

Chapter 5. Exponential and Logarithmic Functions

    a. Greater than0
    c. Undefined
    b. Thing
    d. Undefined

124. In banking and accountancy, the outstanding _____ is the amount of money owned, or due, that remains in a deposit account or a loan account at a given date, after all past remittances, payments and withdrawal have been accounted for.
    a. Thing
    c. Undefined
    b. Balance0
    d. Undefined

125. The _____ of a ring R is defined to be the smallest positive integer n such that n a = 0, for all a in R.
    a. Characteristic0
    c. Undefined
    b. Thing
    d. Undefined

126. In sociology and biology a _____ is the collection of people or organisms of a particular species living in a given geographic area or space, usually measured by a census.
    a. Population0
    c. Undefined
    b. Thing
    d. Undefined

127. _____ is change in population over time, and can be quantified as the change in the number of individuals in a population per unit time.
    a. Population growth0
    c. Undefined
    b. Thing
    d. Undefined

128. A _____ is a set of numbers that designate location in a given reference system, such as x,y in a planar _____ system or an x,y,z in a three-dimensional _____ system.
    a. Coordinate0
    c. Undefined
    b. Thing
    d. Undefined

129. An _____ is when two lines intersect somewhere on a plane creating a right angle at intersection
    a. Thing
    c. Undefined
    b. Axes0
    d. Undefined

130. In a mathematical proof or a syllogism, a _____ is a statement that is the logical consequence of preceding statements.
    a. Conclusion0
    c. Undefined
    b. Concept
    d. Undefined

131. In mathematics, a _____ is a mathematical statement which appears likely to be true, but has not been formally proven to be true under the rules of mathematical logic.
    a. Conjecture0
    c. Undefined
    b. Concept
    d. Undefined

132. In mathematics, the _____ of two sets A and B is the set that contains all elements of A that also belong to B (or equivalently, all elements of B that also belong to A), but no other elements.

Chapter 5. Exponential and Logarithmic Functions 91

    a. Thing   b. Intersection0
    c. Undefined   d. Undefined

133. An _____ is a straight line or curve A to which another curve B approaches closer and closer as one moves along it. As one moves along B, the space between it and the _____ A becomes smaller and smaller, and can in fact be made as small as one could wish by going far enough along. A curve may or may not touch or cross its _____. In fact, the curve may intersect the _____ an infinite number of times.
    a. Thing   b. Asymptote0
    c. Undefined   d. Undefined

134. In mathematics, an _____ number is any real number that is not a rational number- that is, it is a number which cannot be expressed as a fraction m/n, where m and n are integers.
    a. Irrational0   b. Thing
    c. Undefined   d. Undefined

135. In mathematics, an _____ is any real number that is not a rational number ¡ª that is, it is a number which cannot be expressed as m/n, where m and n are integers.
    a. Irrational number0   b. Thing
    c. Undefined   d. Undefined

136. In mathematics, a _____ is an n-tuple with n being 3.
    a. Thing   b. Triple0
    c. Undefined   d. Undefined

137. _____ interest refers to the fact that whenever interest is calculated, it is based not only on the original principal, but also on any unpaid interest that has been added to the principal.
    a. Thing   b. Compound0
    c. Undefined   d. Undefined

138. _____ refers to the fact that whenever interest is calculated, it is based not only on the original principal, but also on any unpaid interest that has been added to the principal. The more frequently interest is compounded, the faster the balance grows.
    a. Compound interest0   b. Concept
    c. Undefined   d. Undefined

139. _____ or investing is a term with several closely-related meanings in business management, finance and economics, related to saving or deferring consumption.
    a. Investment0   b. Thing
    c. Undefined   d. Undefined

140. _____ is the chance that something is likely to happen or be the case.
    a. Thing   b. Probability0
    c. Undefined   d. Undefined

141. In elementary algebra, an _____ is a set that contains every real number between two indicated numbers and may contain the two numbers themselves.

Chapter 5. Exponential and Logarithmic Functions

    a. Interval0
    b. Thing
    c. Undefined
    d. Undefined

142. In mathematics, a _____ is a two-dimensional manifold or surface that is perfectly flat.
    a. Thing
    b. Plane0
    c. Undefined
    d. Undefined

143. In economics _____ means before deductions brutto, e.g. _____ domestic or national product, or _____ profit or income
    a. Thing
    b. Gross0
    c. Undefined
    d. Undefined

144. Transport or _____ is the movement of people and goods from one place to another.
    a. Transportation0
    b. Thing
    c. Undefined
    d. Undefined

145. _____ is mass m per unit volume V.
    a. Thing
    b. Density0
    c. Undefined
    d. Undefined

146. In Euclidean geometry, a _____ is the set of all points in a plane at a fixed distance, called the radius, from a given point, the center.
    a. Thing
    b. Circle0
    c. Undefined
    d. Undefined

147. In mathematics, the conjugate _____ or adjoint matrix of an m-by-n matrix A with complex entries is the n-by-m matrix A* obtained from A by taking the transpose and then taking the complex conjugate of each entry.
    a. Thing
    b. Pairs0
    c. Undefined
    d. Undefined

148. _____ of a single or multiple future payments is the nominal amounts of money to change hands at some future date, discounted to account for the time value of money, and other factors such as investment risk.
    a. Thing
    b. Present value0
    c. Undefined
    d. Undefined

149. _____ measures the nominal future sum of money that a given sum of money is "worth" at a specified time in the future assuming a certain interest rate; this value does not include corrections for inflation or other factors that affect the true value of money in the future.
    a. Future value0
    b. Thing
    c. Undefined
    d. Undefined

150. In mathematics, the _____ is the logarithm with base 10.
    a. Thing
    b. Common logarithm0
    c. Undefined
    d. Undefined

Chapter 5. Exponential and Logarithmic Functions

151. In mathematics, a _____ of a number x is the exponent y of the power by such that $x = b^y$. The value used for the base b must be neither 0 nor 1, nor a root of 1 in the case of the extension to complex numbers, and is typically 10, e, or 2.
 a. Logarithm0
 b. Thing
 c. Undefined
 d. Undefined

152. In mathematics, a _____ of a number x is a number r such that $r^2 = x$, or in words, a number r whose square (the result of multiplying the number by itself) is x.
 a. Thing
 b. Square root0
 c. Undefined
 d. Undefined

153. A _____ is a number that is less than zero.
 a. Thing
 b. Negative number0
 c. Undefined
 d. Undefined

154. A _____ is a negotiable instrument instructing a financial institution to pay a specific amount of a specific currency from a specific demand account held in the maker/depositor's name with that institution. Both the maker and payee may be natural persons or legal entities.
 a. Check0
 b. Thing
 c. Undefined
 d. Undefined

155. The _____ relative to a specified or implied reference level.
 a. Decibel0
 b. Thing
 c. Undefined
 d. Undefined

156. _____ is a trigonemtric function that is important when studying triangles and modeling periodic phenomena, among other applications.
 a. Thing
 b. Sine0
 c. Undefined
 d. Undefined

157. In mathematics, a _____ is a countable collection of open covers of a topological space that satisfies certain separation axioms.
 a. Development0
 b. Thing
 c. Undefined
 d. Undefined

158. _____ is the logarithm to the base e, where e is an irrational constant approximately equal to 2.718281828459.
 a. Thing
 b. Natural logarithm0
 c. Undefined
 d. Undefined

159. _____ is the notation in which permitted values for a variable are expressed as ranging over a certain interval; "5 < x < 9" is an example of the application of _____.
 a. Interval notation0
 b. Thing
 c. Undefined
 d. Undefined

160. _____ is a straight line or curve A to which another curve B the one being studied approaches closer and closer as one moves along it.

Chapter 5. Exponential and Logarithmic Functions

a. Vertical asymptote0
b. Thing
c. Undefined
d. Undefined

161. In mathematics, _____ are two-dimensional manifolds or surfaces that are perfectly flat.
    a. Planes0
    b. Thing
    c. Undefined
    d. Undefined

162. In Euclidean geometry, a uniform _____ is a linear transformation that enlargers or diminishes objects, and whose _____ factor is the same in all directions. This is also called homothethy.
    a. Thing
    b. Scale0
    c. Undefined
    d. Undefined

163. An _____ is the result from the sudden release of stored energy in the Earth's crust that creates seismic waves.
    a. Earthquake0
    b. Thing
    c. Undefined
    d. Undefined

164. The _____ of a mathematical object is its size: a property by which it can be larger or smaller than other objects of the same kind; in technical terms, an ordering of the class of objects to which it belongs.
    a. Magnitude0
    b. Thing
    c. Undefined
    d. Undefined

165. _____, or tropical cyclones are meterological terms for a storm system characterized by a low pressure center and thunderstorms that produces strong wind and flooding rain.
    a. Thing
    b. Hurricanes0
    c. Undefined
    d. Undefined

166. _____ is a term applied when talking about the movement of air from one place to the next.
    a. Thing
    b. Wind speed0
    c. Undefined
    d. Undefined

167. The metre (or _____, see spelling differences) is a measure of length. It is the basic unit of length in the metric system and in the International System of Units (SI), used around the world for general and scientific purposes.
    a. Concept
    b. Meter0
    c. Undefined
    d. Undefined

168. Sir Isaac _____, was an English physicist, mathematician, astronomer, natural philosopher, and alchemist, regarded by many as the greatest figure in the history of science
    a. Person
    b. Newton0
    c. Undefined
    d. Undefined

169. _____ algebra (sometimes called General algebra) is the field of mathematics that studies the ideas common to all algebraic structures.
    a. Universal0
    b. Thing
    c. Undefined
    d. Undefined

Chapter 5. Exponential and Logarithmic Functions 95

170. _____ was a German Lutheran mathematician, astronomer and astrologer, and a key figure in the 17th century astronomical revolution.
 a. Person
 b. Johannes Kepler0
 c. Undefined
 d. Undefined

171. Sir _____ was an English physicist, mathematician, astronomer, natural philosopher, and alchemist, regarded by many as the greatest figure in the history of science.
 a. Person
 b. Isaac Newton0
 c. Undefined
 d. Undefined

172. In mathematics and logic, a _____ proof is a way of showing the truth or falsehood of a given statement by a straightforward combination of established facts, usually existing lemmas and theorems, without making any further assumptions.
 a. Thing
 b. Direct0
 c. Undefined
 d. Undefined

173. The _____ is the process of converting elements in one basis to another when both describe the same elements of the finite field GF(p^m).
 a. Change of base0
 b. Thing
 c. Undefined
 d. Undefined

174. The _____ is the process of converting elements in one basis to another when both describe the same elements of the finite field GF(p^m).
 a. Change of bases0
 b. Thing
 c. Undefined
 d. Undefined

175. An _____ is an equality that remains true regardless of the values of any variables that appear within it, to distinguish it from an equality which is true under more particular conditions.
 a. Identity0
 b. Thing
 c. Undefined
 d. Undefined

176. The population _____ is the total number of human beings alive on the planet Earth at a given time.
 a. Of the world0
 b. Thing
 c. Undefined
 d. Undefined

177. The _____ is the total number of human beings alive on the planet Earth at a given time.
 a. World population0
 b. Thing
 c. Undefined
 d. Undefined

178. In mathematics, a _____ number (or a _____) is a natural number that has exactly two (distinct) natural number divisors, which are 1 and the _____ number itself.
 a. Thing
 b. Prime0
 c. Undefined
 d. Undefined

179. _____ (Groups, Algorithms and Programming) is a computer algebra system for computational discrete algebra with particular emphasis on, but not restricted to, computational group theory.

Chapter 5. Exponential and Logarithmic Functions

a. Gap0
b. Thing
c. Undefined
d. Undefined

180. The deductive-nomological model is a formalized view of scientific _____ in natural language.
    a. Explanation0
    b. Thing
    c. Undefined
    d. Undefined

181. A _____ is a system of payment named after the small plastic card issued to users of the system.
    a. Thing
    b. Credit card0
    c. Undefined
    d. Undefined

182. In geometry, an _____ of a triangle is a straight line through a vertex and perpendicular to (i.e. forming a right angle with) the opposite side or an extension of the opposite side.
    a. Concept
    b. Altitude0
    c. Undefined
    d. Undefined

183. _____, usually denoted symbolically by the Greek letter phi, φ, gives the location of a place on Earth north or south of the equator. _____ is an angular measurement in degrees (marked with °) ranging from 0° at the Equator (low _____) to 90° at the poles (90° N for the North Pole or 90° S for the South Pole; high _____). The complementary angle of a _____ is called the colatitude.
    a. Thing
    b. Latitude0
    c. Undefined
    d. Undefined

184. The _____ or kilogramme is the SI base unit of mass. It is defined as being equal to the mass of the international prototype of the _____.
    a. Kilogram0
    b. Thing
    c. Undefined
    d. Undefined

185. In mathematics, _____ refers to the rewriting of an expression into a simpler form.
    a. Reduction0
    b. Thing
    c. Undefined
    d. Undefined

186. _____ systems represent systems whose behavior is not expressible as a sum of the behaviors of its descriptors.
    a. Nonlinear0
    b. Thing
    c. Undefined
    d. Undefined

187. A _____ models the S-curve of growth of some set P. The initial stage of growth is approximately exponential; then, as saturation begins, the growth slows, and at maturity, growth stops.
    a. Thing
    b. Logistic function0
    c. Undefined
    d. Undefined

188. A _____, scatter diagram or scatter graph is a graph used in statistics to visually display and relate two quantitative variables of a multidimensional data set by displaying the data as a collection of points, each having one coordinate on a horizontal and one on a vertical axis.

Chapter 5. Exponential and Logarithmic Functions

    a. Thing
    b. Scatterplot0
    c. Undefined
    d. Undefined

189. In mathematics, the concept of a _____ tries to capture the intuitive idea of a geometrical one-dimensional and continuous object. A simple example is the circle.
    a. Thing
    b. Curve0
    c. Undefined
    d. Undefined

190. _____ is the level of functional and/or metabolic efficiency of an organism at both the micro level.
    a. Health0
    b. Thing
    c. Undefined
    d. Undefined

191. _____ is the interdisciplinary scientific study of the atmosphere that focuses on weather processes and forecasting.
    a. Meteorology0
    b. Thing
    c. Undefined
    d. Undefined

192. A _____ is a unit of length in the metric system, equal to one thousand metres, the current SI base unit of length
    a. Kilometer0
    b. Thing
    c. Undefined
    d. Undefined

193. _____, symbol km^2, are decimal multiples of SI unit of surface area square metre, one of the SI derived units.
    a. Thing
    b. Square kilometers0
    c. Undefined
    d. Undefined

194. _____ primarily refers to social welfare service concerned with social protection, or protection against socially recognized conditions, including poverty, old age, disability, unemployment, families with children and others.
    a. Social security0
    b. Thing
    c. Undefined
    d. Undefined

195. A _____ of a number is the product of that number with any integer.
    a. Thing
    b. Multiple0
    c. Undefined
    d. Undefined

196. _____ is the flow of blood in the cardiovascular system.
    a. Blood flow0
    b. Thing
    c. Undefined
    d. Undefined

197. _____ is the process in which two clone daughter cells are produced by the cell division of one bacterium.
    a. Bacteria growth0
    b. Thing
    c. Undefined
    d. Undefined

198. _____ is a mathematical science pertaining to the collection, analysis, interpretation or explanation, and presentation of data. It is applicable to a wide variety of academic disciplines, from the physical and social sciences to the humanities.

Chapter 5. Exponential and Logarithmic Functions

a. Thing
b. Statistics0
c. Undefined
d. Undefined

199. In topology and related areas of mathematics a _____ or Moore-Smith sequence is a generalization of a sequence, intended to unify the various notions of limit and generalize them to arbitrary topological spaces.
a. Thing
b. Net0
c. Undefined
d. Undefined

200. _____ is the process of recording pictures by means of capturing light on a light-sensitive medium, such as a film or sensor.
a. Photography0
b. Thing
c. Undefined
d. Undefined

201. The payment of _____ as remuneration for services rendered or products sold is a common way to reward sales people.
a. Thing
b. Commission0
c. Undefined
d. Undefined

202. _____ are procedures that allow people to exchange information by one of several methods.
a. Communications0
b. Thing
c. Undefined
d. Undefined

203. _____ is an adjective usually refering to being in the centre.
a. Central0
b. Thing
c. Undefined
d. Undefined

Chapter 6. Systems of Equations and Inequalities

1. A _____ is a symbolic representation denoting a quantity or expression. It often represents an "unknown" quantity that has the potential to change.
   a. Thing
   b. Variable0
   c. Undefined
   d. Undefined

2. The mathematical concept of a _____ expresses the intuitive idea of deterministic dependence between two quantities, one of which is viewed as primary and the other as secondary. A _____ then is a way to associate a unique output for each input of a specified type, for example, a real number or an element of a given set.
   a. Thing
   b. Function0
   c. Undefined
   d. Undefined

3. _____ is a term applied when talking about the movement of air from one place to the next.
   a. Wind speed0
   b. Thing
   c. Undefined
   d. Undefined

4. The word _____ is used in a variety of ways in mathematics.
   a. Index0
   b. Thing
   c. Undefined
   d. Undefined

5. _____ is a physical property of a system that underlies the common notions of hot and cold; something that is hotter has the greater _____.
   a. Thing
   b. Temperature0
   c. Undefined
   d. Undefined

6. In mathematics, an _____, mean, or central tendency of a data set refers to a measure of the "middle" or "expected" value of the data set.
   a. Concept
   b. Average0
   c. Undefined
   d. Undefined

7. In mathematics, _____ is an elementary arithmetic operation. When one of the numbers is a whole number, _____ is the repeated sum of the other number.
   a. Multiplication0
   b. Thing
   c. Undefined
   d. Undefined

8. _____ or arithmetics is the oldest and most elementary branch of mathematics, used by almost everyone, for tasks ranging from simple daily counting to advanced science and business calculations.
   a. Thing
   b. Arithmetic0
   c. Undefined
   d. Undefined

9. The traditional _____ are addition, subtraction, multiplication and division, although more advanced operations (such as manipulations of percentages, square root, exponentiation, and logarithmic functions) are also sometimes included in this subject.
   a. Arithmetic operations0
   b. Concept
   c. Undefined
   d. Undefined

10. In mathematics, an _____ is any of the arguments, i.e. "inputs", to a function. Thus if we have a function f(x), then x is a _____.

a. Thing
b. Independent variable0
c. Undefined
d. Undefined

11. In a function the _____, is the variable which is the value, i.e. the "output", of the function.
a. Dependent variable0
b. Thing
c. Undefined
d. Undefined

12. The _____ of a solid object is the three-dimensional concept of how much space it occupies, often quantified numerically.
a. Thing
b. Volume0
c. Undefined
d. Undefined

13. In classical geometry, a _____ of a circle or sphere is any line segment from its center to its boundary. By extension, the _____ of a circle or sphere is the length of any such segment. The _____ is half the diameter. In science and engineering the term _____ of curvature is commonly used as a synonym for _____.
a. Thing
b. Radius0
c. Undefined
d. Undefined

14. U.S. liquid _____ is legally defined as 231 cubic inches, and is equal to 3.785411784 litres or abotu 0.13368 cubic feet. This is the most common definition of a _____. The U.S. fluid ounce is defined as 1/128 of a U.S. _____.
a. Gallon0
b. Thing
c. Undefined
d. Undefined

15. _____ is the transport of people on a trip/journey or the process or time involved in a person or object moving from one location to another.
a. Thing
b. Travel0
c. Undefined
d. Undefined

16. A _____ is a unit of length, usually used to measure distance, in a number of different systems, including Imperial units, United States customary units and Norwegian/Swedish mil. Its size can vary from system to system, but in each is between 1 and 10 kilometers. In contemporary English contexts _____ refers to either:
a. Thing
b. Mile0
c. Undefined
d. Undefined

17. The _____ or kilogramme is the SI base unit of mass. It is defined as being equal to the mass of the international prototype of the _____.
a. Kilogram0
b. Thing
c. Undefined
d. Undefined

18. In plane geometry, a _____ is a polygon with four equal sides, four right angles, and parallel opposite sides. In algebra, the _____ of a number is that number multiplied by itself.
a. Thing
b. Square0
c. Undefined
d. Undefined

Chapter 6. Systems of Equations and Inequalities

19. The act of _____ is the calculated approximation of a result which is usable even if input data may be incomplete, uncertain, or noisy.
    a. Estimating0
    b. Thing
    c. Undefined
    d. Undefined

20. The metre (or _____, see spelling differences) is a measure of length. It is the basic unit of length in the metric system and in the International System of Units (SI), used around the world for general and scientific purposes.
    a. Meter0
    b. Concept
    c. Undefined
    d. Undefined

21. In Euclidean geometry, a _____ is the set of all points in a plane at a fixed distance, called the radius, from a given point, the center.
    a. Circle0
    b. Thing
    c. Undefined
    d. Undefined

22. _____ is the distance around a given two-dimensional object. As a general rule, the _____ of a polygon can always be calculated by adding all the length of the sides together. So, the formula for triangles is P = a + b + c, where a, b and c stand for each side of it. For quadrilaterals the equation is P = a + b + c + d. For equilateral polygons, P = na, where n is the number of sides and a is the side length.
    a. Perimeter0
    b. Thing
    c. Undefined
    d. Undefined

23. The word _____ comes from the Latin word linearis, which means created by lines.
    a. Thing
    b. Linear0
    c. Undefined
    d. Undefined

24. A _____ is an equation in which each term is either a constant or the product of a constant times the first power of a variable.
    a. Thing
    b. Linear equation0
    c. Undefined
    d. Undefined

25. A _____ is a set of possible values that a variable can take on in order to satisfy a given set of conditions, which may include equations and inequalities.
    a. Solution set0
    b. Thing
    c. Undefined
    d. Undefined

26. _____ systems represent systems whose behavior is not expressible as a sum of the behaviors of its descriptors.
    a. Nonlinear0
    b. Thing
    c. Undefined
    d. Undefined

27. _____ are a set of equations containing multiple variables.
    a. Thing
    b. Systems of equations0
    c. Undefined
    d. Undefined

Chapter 6. Systems of Equations and Inequalities

28. A _____ is a negotiable instrument instructing a financial institution to pay a specific amount of a specific currency from a specific demand account held in the maker/depositor's name with that institution. Both the maker and payee may be natural persons or legal entities.
   a. Thing
   b. Check0
   c. Undefined
   d. Undefined

29. In economics _____ means before deductions brutto, e.g. _____ domestic or national product, or _____ profit or income
   a. Thing
   b. Gross0
   c. Undefined
   d. Undefined

30. _____ is a branch of mathematics concerning the study of structure, relation and quantity.
   a. Algebra0
   b. Concept
   c. Undefined
   d. Undefined

31. An _____ is a collection of two not necessarily distinct objects, one of which is distinguished as the first coordinate and the other as the second coordinate.
   a. Thing
   b. Ordered pair0
   c. Undefined
   d. Undefined

32. In mathematics, _____ is the decomposition of an object into a product of other objects, or factors, which when multiplied together give the original.
   a. Thing
   b. Factoring0
   c. Undefined
   d. Undefined

33. In mathematics, the _____ of a coordinate system is the point where the axes of the system intersect.
   a. Origin0
   b. Thing
   c. Undefined
   d. Undefined

34. _____ are the basic objects of study in graph theory. Informally speaking, a graph is a set of objects called points, nodes, or vertices connected by links called lines or edges.
   a. Thing
   b. Graphs0
   c. Undefined
   d. Undefined

35. A _____ represents a system whose behavior is not expressible as a sum of the behaviors of its descriptors.
   a. Nonlinear system0
   b. Thing
   c. Undefined
   d. Undefined

36. In mathematics, the _____ is a conic section generated by the intersection of a right circular conical surface and a plane parallel to a generating straight line of that surface. It can also be defined as locus of points in a plane which are equidistant from a given point.
   a. Thing
   b. Parabola0
   c. Undefined
   d. Undefined

37. An _____ is an equality that remains true regardless of the values of any variables that appear within it, to distinguish it from an equality which is true under more particular conditions.

Chapter 6. Systems of Equations and Inequalities

    a. Thing
    b. Identity0
    c. Undefined
    d. Undefined

38. A _____ is a set of numbers that designate location in a given reference system, such as x,y in a planar _____ system or an x,y,z in a three-dimensional _____ system.
    a. Thing
    b. Coordinate0
    c. Undefined
    d. Undefined

39. In architecture and structural engineering, a _____ is a structure comprizing one or more triangular units which are constructed with straight slender members whose ends are connected at joints.
    a. Truss0
    b. Thing
    c. Undefined
    d. Undefined

40. In physics, _____ is an influence that may cause an object to accelerate. It may be experienced as a lift, a push, or a pull. The actual acceleration of the body is determined by the vector sum of all forces acting on it, known as net _____ or resultant _____.
    a. Thing
    b. Force0
    c. Undefined
    d. Undefined

41. In mathematics, a _____ is a quadric surface, with the following equation in Cartesian coordinates: $(x/_a)^2 + (y/_b)^2 = 1$.
    a. Thing
    b. Cylinder0
    c. Undefined
    d. Undefined

42. _____ the expected value of a random variable displays the average or central value of the variable. It is a summary value of the distribution of the variable.
    a. Thing
    b. Determining0
    c. Undefined
    d. Undefined

43. A _____ surface is the surface or face of a solid on its sides. It can also be defined as any face or surface that is not a base.
    a. Lateral0
    b. Thing
    c. Undefined
    d. Undefined

44. In mathematics, the _____ of two sets A and B is the set that contains all elements of A that also belong to B (or equivalently, all elements of B that also belong to A), but no other elements.
    a. Intersection0
    b. Thing
    c. Undefined
    d. Undefined

45. _____ is a relationship among three or more variables in which each pair of variables varies directly or inversely.
    a. Joint variation0
    b. Thing
    c. Undefined
    d. Undefined

46. _____ is a kind of property which exists as magnitude or multitude. It is among the basic classes of things along with quality, substance, change, and relation.

Chapter 6. Systems of Equations and Inequalities

a. Thing
b. Amount0
c. Undefined
d. Undefined

47. In geometry, a _____ (Greek words diairo = divide and metro = measure) of a circle is any straight line segment that passes through the centre and whose endpoints are on the circular boundary, or, in more modern usage, the length of such a line segment. When using the word in the more modern sense, one speaks of the _____ rather than a _____, because all diameters of a circle have the same length. This length is twice the radius. The _____ of a circle is also the longest chord that the circle has.
a. Diameter0
b. Thing
c. Undefined
d. Undefined

48. _____ has many meanings, most of which simply .
a. Power0
b. Thing
c. Undefined
d. Undefined

49. In mathematics and the mathematical sciences, a _____ is a fixed, but possibly unspecified, value. This is in contrast to a variable, which is not fixed.
a. Thing
b. Constant0
c. Undefined
d. Undefined

50. In mathematics, a _____ of a number x is a number r such that r^2 = x, or in words, a number r whose square (the result of multiplying the number by itself) is x.
a. Square root0
b. Thing
c. Undefined
d. Undefined

51. A _____ is the result of the addition of a set of numbers. The numbers may be natural numbers, complex numbers, matrices, or still more complicated objects. An infinite _____ is a subtle procedure known as a series.
a. Sum0
b. Thing
c. Undefined
d. Undefined

52. In mathematics, a _____ of a complex-valued function f is a member x of the domain of f such that f(x) vanishes at x, that is, x : f (x) = 0.
a. Root0
b. Thing
c. Undefined
d. Undefined

53. In mathematics, the conjugate _____ or adjoint matrix of an m-by-n matrix A with complex entries is the n-by-m matrix A* obtained from A by taking the transpose and then taking the complex conjugate of each entry.
a. Pairs0
b. Thing
c. Undefined
d. Undefined

54. In geometry, a _____ is defined as a quadrilateral where all four of its angles are right angles.
a. Thing
b. Rectangle0
c. Undefined
d. Undefined

55. _____ is a state located in the southern and southwestern regions of the United States of America.

Chapter 6. Systems of Equations and Inequalities

    a. Thing
    b. Texas0
    c. Undefined
    d. Undefined

56. A _____ is a special kind of ratio, indicating a relationship between two measurements with different units, such as miles to gallons or cents to pounds.
    a. Thing
    b. Rate0
    c. Undefined
    d. Undefined

57. _____ is a subset of a population.
    a. Thing
    b. Sample0
    c. Undefined
    d. Undefined

58. _____ is the fee paid on borrowed money.
    a. Thing
    b. Interest0
    c. Undefined
    d. Undefined

59. An _____ is the fee paid on borrow money.
    a. Concept
    b. Interest rate0
    c. Undefined
    d. Undefined

60. In mathematics, a _____ is a two-dimensional manifold or surface that is perfectly flat.
    a. Plane0
    b. Thing
    c. Undefined
    d. Undefined

61. _____ are a measure of time.
    a. Thing
    b. Minutes0
    c. Undefined
    d. Undefined

62. A _____ is a three-dimensional solid object bounded by six square faces, facets, or sides, with three meeting at each vertex.
    a. Cube0
    b. Thing
    c. Undefined
    d. Undefined

63. A _____ of a number is a number a such that $a^3 = x$.
    a. Thing
    b. Cube root0
    c. Undefined
    d. Undefined

64. _____ of an object is its speed in a particular direction.
    a. Thing
    b. Velocity0
    c. Undefined
    d. Undefined

65. An _____ is a combination of numbers, operators, grouping symbols and/or free variables and bound variables arranged in a meaningful way which can be evaluated..
    a. Thing
    b. Expression0
    c. Undefined
    d. Undefined

Chapter 6. Systems of Equations and Inequalities

66. _____ is electromagnetic radiation with a wavelength that is visible to the eye (visible _____) or, in a technical or scientific context, electromagnetic radiation of any wavelength.
- a. Light0
- b. Thing
- c. Undefined
- d. Undefined

67. In mathematics, a _____ is a mathematical statement which appears likely to be true, but has not been formally proven to be true under the rules of mathematical logic.
- a. Conjecture0
- b. Concept
- c. Undefined
- d. Undefined

68. The Gaussian _____ is an algorithm which can be used to determine the solutions of a system of linear equations, to find the rank of a matrix, and to calculate the inverse of an invertible square matrix.
- a. Thing
- b. Elimination method0
- c. Undefined
- d. Undefined

69. In mathematics, _____ problems involve the optimization of a linear objective function, subject to linear equality and inequality constraints.
- a. Linear programming0
- b. Thing
- c. Undefined
- d. Undefined

70. In mathematics, an _____ is a statement about the relative size or order of two objects.
- a. Thing
- b. Inequality0
- c. Undefined
- d. Undefined

71. The existence and properties of _____ are the basis of Euclid's parallel postulate. _____ are two lines on the same plane that do not intersect even assuming that lines extend to infinity in either direction.
- a. Thing
- b. Parallel lines0
- c. Undefined
- d. Undefined

72. The _____ is used to discard one of the variables in an equation, only to replace it with the actual value when solving multiple equations.
- a. Substitution method0
- b. Thing
- c. Undefined
- d. Undefined

73. Equivalence is the condition of being _____ or essentially equal.
- a. Equivalent0
- b. Thing
- c. Undefined
- d. Undefined

74. _____ are activities that are governed by a set of rules or customs and often engaged in competitively.
- a. Sports0
- b. Thing
- c. Undefined
- d. Undefined

75. In common philosophical language, a proposition or _____, is the content of an assertion, that is, it is true-or-false and defined by the meaning of a particular piece of language.

Chapter 6. Systems of Equations and Inequalities

    a. Concept
    c. Undefined
    b. Statement0
    d. Undefined

76. Acid _____ ratio measures the ability of a company to use its near cash or quick assets to immediately extinguish its current liabilities.
    a. Test0
    c. Undefined
    b. Thing
    d. Undefined

77. In mathematics, the concept of a _____ tries to capture the intuitive idea of a geometrical one-dimensional and continuous object. A simple example is the circle.
    a. Thing
    c. Undefined
    b. Curve0
    d. Undefined

78. In topology, the _____ are subsets S of a topological space X is the set of points which can be approached both from S and from the outside of S.
    a. Boundaries0
    c. Undefined
    b. Thing
    d. Undefined

79. Two mathematical objects are equal if and only if they are precisely the same in every way. This defines a binary relation, _____, denoted by the sign of _____ "=" in such a way that the statement "x = y" means that x and y are equal.
    a. Equality0
    c. Undefined
    b. Thing
    d. Undefined

80. In mathematics, _____ geometry was the traditional name for the geometry of three-dimensional Euclidean space — for practical purposes the kind of space we live in.
    a. Thing
    c. Undefined
    b. Solid0
    d. Undefined

81. An _____ or member of a set is an object that when collected together make up the set.
    a. Element0
    c. Undefined
    b. Thing
    d. Undefined

82. In mathematics, the _____, or members of a set or more generally a class are all those objects which when collected together make up the set or class.
    a. Thing
    c. Undefined
    b. Elements0
    d. Undefined

83. _____ is the interdisciplinary scientific study of the atmosphere that focuses on weather processes and forecasting.
    a. Thing
    c. Undefined
    b. Meteorology0
    d. Undefined

84. _____ is a state in both the Midwestern and Western regions of the United States of America. It is the northernmost of the Great Plains states and is the northern half of The Dakotas.

Chapter 6. Systems of Equations and Inequalities

  a. North Dakota0
  b. Thing
  c. Undefined
  d. Undefined

85. _____, from Latin meaning "to make progress", is defined in two different ways. Pure economic _____ is the increase in wealth that an investor has from making an investment, taking into consideration all costs associated with that investment including the opportunity cost of capital.
  a. Profit0
  b. Thing
  c. Undefined
  d. Undefined

86. In economics, supply and _____ describe market relations between prospective sellers and buyers of a good.
  a. Demand0
  b. Thing
  c. Undefined
  d. Undefined

87. In mathematics, a _____ is a condition that a solution to an optimization problem must satisfy in order to be acceptable.
  a. Thing
  b. Constraint0
  c. Undefined
  d. Undefined

88. In geometry, a _____ is a special kind of point, usually a corner of a polygon, polyhedron, or higher dimensional polytope. In the geometry of curves a _____ is a point of where the first derivative of curvature is zero. In graph theory, a _____ is the fundamental unit out of which graphs are formed
  a. Vertex0
  b. Thing
  c. Undefined
  d. Undefined

89. In mathematics, a _____ is a statement that can be proved on the basis of explicitly stated or previously agreed assumptions.
  a. Theorem0
  b. Thing
  c. Undefined
  d. Undefined

90. In number theory, the _____ of arithmetic (or unique factorization theorem) states that every natural number greater than 1 can be written as a unique product of prime numbers.
  a. Fundamental theorem0
  b. Concept
  c. Undefined
  d. Undefined

91. In chemistry, a _____ is substance made by combining two or more different materials in such a way that no chemical reaction occurs.
  a. Mixture0
  b. Thing
  c. Undefined
  d. Undefined

92. In geometry, _____ lines are two lines that share one or more common points.
  a. Intersecting0
  b. Thing
  c. Undefined
  d. Undefined

93. In mathematics and more specifically set theory, the _____ set is the unique set which contains no elements.

Chapter 6. Systems of Equations and Inequalities

    a. Thing
    b. Empty0
    c. Undefined
    d. Undefined

94. A _____ is a type of debt. All material things can be lent but this article focuses exclusively on monetary loans. Like all debt instruments, a _____ entails the redistribution of financial assets over time, between the lender and the borrower.
    a. Loan0
    b. Thing
    c. Undefined
    d. Undefined

95. _____ is the general term that is used to describe physical artifacts of a technology.
    a. Hardware0
    b. Thing
    c. Undefined
    d. Undefined

96. In mathematics, a _____ is an n-tuple with n being 3.
    a. Triple0
    b. Thing
    c. Undefined
    d. Undefined

97. In Graph theory, a _____ is a digraph with weighted edges.
    a. Network0
    b. Concept
    c. Undefined
    d. Undefined

98. _____ is the speed of an aircraft relative to the air.
    a. Airspeed0
    b. Thing
    c. Undefined
    d. Undefined

99. In combinatorial mathematics, a _____ is an un-ordered collection of unique elements.
    a. Combination0
    b. Concept
    c. Undefined
    d. Undefined

100. The _____ of measurement are a globally standardized and modernized form of the metric system.
    a. Thing
    b. Units0
    c. Undefined
    d. Undefined

101. _____ is a business term for the amount of money that a company receives from its activities in a given period, mostly from sales of products and/or services to customers
    a. Revenue0
    b. Thing
    c. Undefined
    d. Undefined

102. _____ is a set, with some particular properties and usually some additional structure, such as the operations of addition or multiplication, for instance.
    a. Thing
    b. Space0
    c. Undefined
    d. Undefined

103. _____ is the ability to hold, receive or absorb, or a measure thereof, similar to the concept of volume.

Chapter 6. Systems of Equations and Inequalities

   a. Concept
   c. Undefined
   b. Capacity0
   d. Undefined

104. One of the three formats applicable to a quadratic function is the _____ which is defined as $f = ax^2 + bx + c$.
   a. General form0
   c. Undefined
   b. Thing
   d. Undefined

105. The _____, the average in everyday English, which is also called the arithmetic _____ (and is distinguished from the geometric _____ or harmonic _____). The average is also called the sample _____. The expected value of a random variable, which is also called the population _____.
   a. Thing
   c. Undefined
   b. Mean0
   d. Undefined

106. In set theory and other branches of mathematics, the _____ of a collection of sets is the set that contains everything that belongs to any of the sets, but nothing else.
   a. Union0
   c. Undefined
   b. Thing
   d. Undefined

107. The deductive-nomological model is a formalized view of scientific _____ in natural language.
   a. Explanation0
   c. Undefined
   b. Thing
   d. Undefined

108. A _____ is one of the basic shapes of geometry: a polygon with three vertices and three sides which are straight line segments.
   a. Triangle0
   c. Undefined
   b. Thing
   d. Undefined

109. A _____ is a function that assigns a number to subsets of a given set.
   a. Thing
   c. Undefined
   b. Measure0
   d. Undefined

110. A _____ is a form of collective investment that pools money from many investors and invests their money in stocks, bonds, short-term money market instruments, and/or other securities.
   a. Thing
   c. Undefined
   b. Mutual fund0
   d. Undefined

111. _____ or investing is a term with several closely-related meanings in business management, finance and economics, related to saving or deferring consumption.
   a. Thing
   c. Undefined
   b. Investment0
   d. Undefined

112. Johann _____ was a German mathematician and scientist of profound genius who contributed significantly to many fields, including number theory, analysis, differential geometry, geodesy, magnetism, astronomy, and optics. He completed Disquisitiones Arithmeticae, his magnum opus, at the age of twenty-one.

Chapter 6. Systems of Equations and Inequalities

   a. Person
   c. Undefined
   b. Carl Friedrich Gauss0
   d. Undefined

113. In mathematics, a _____ is a rectangular table of numbers or, more generally, a table consisting of abstract quantities that can be added and multiplied.
   a. Matrix0
   c. Undefined
   b. Thing
   d. Undefined

114. _____ are rectangular tables (or grids) of information, often financial information.
   a. Spreadsheets0
   c. Undefined
   b. Thing
   d. Undefined

115. _____ is a synonym for information.
   a. Thing
   c. Undefined
   b. Data0
   d. Undefined

116. In mathematics, a matrix can be thought of as each row or _____ being a vector. Hence, a space formed by row vectors or _____ vectors are said to be a row space or a _____ space.
   a. Column0
   c. Undefined
   b. Concept
   d. Undefined

117. In mathematics, a _____ is a constant multiplicative factor of a certain object. The object can be such things as a variable, a vector, a function, etc. For example, the _____ of $9x^2$ is 9.
   a. Thing
   c. Undefined
   b. Coefficient0
   d. Undefined

118. In linear algebra, the _____ refers to a matrix consisting of the coefficients of the variables in a set of linear equations.
   a. Thing
   c. Undefined
   b. Coefficient matrix0
   d. Undefined

119. In linear algebra, the _____ of a matrix is obtained by combining two matrices in such a way that a matrix of coefficients to which has been added a column of constants corresponds to the right hand side of the equations.
   a. Augmented matrix0
   c. Undefined
   b. Thing
   d. Undefined

120. _____ is an algorithm which can be used to determine the solutions of a system of linear equations, to find the rank of a matrix, and to calculate the inverse of an invertible square matrix.
   a. Thing
   c. Undefined
   b. Gaussian elimination0
   d. Undefined

121. In linear algebra, the _____ of a square matrix is the diagonal which runs from the top left corner to the bottom right corner.
   a. Thing
   c. Undefined
   b. Main diagonal0
   d. Undefined

Chapter 6. Systems of Equations and Inequalities

122. A _____ can refer to a line joining two nonadjacent vertices of a polygon or polyhedron, or in some contexts any upward or downward sloping line. .
- a. Diagonal0
- b. Thing
- c. Undefined
- d. Undefined

123. In mathematics, a _____ may be described informally as a number that can be given by an infinite decimal representation.
- a. Real number0
- b. Thing
- c. Undefined
- d. Undefined

124. A _____ is the quantity that defines certain relatively constant characteristics of systems or functions..
- a. Thing
- b. Parameter0
- c. Undefined
- d. Undefined

125. A _____ of a number is the product of that number with any integer.
- a. Multiple0
- b. Thing
- c. Undefined
- d. Undefined

126. Initial objects are also called _____, and terminal objects are also called final.
- a. Thing
- b. Coterminal0
- c. Undefined
- d. Undefined

127. A _____ is a one-dimensional picture in which the integers are shown as specially-marked points evenly spaced on a line.
- a. Number line0
- b. Thing
- c. Undefined
- d. Undefined

128. A _____ is a polynomial function of the form $f(x) = ax^2 + bx + c$, where a, b, c are real numbers and a , 0.
- a. Event
- b. Quadratic function0
- c. Undefined
- d. Undefined

129. In computer science an _____ is a data structure that consists of a group of elements having a single name that are accessed by indexing. In most programming languages each element has the same data type and the _____ occupies a continuous area of storage.
- a. Thing
- b. Array0
- c. Undefined
- d. Undefined

130. In mathematics, a _____ is an ordered list of objects. Like a set, it contains members, also called elements or terms, and the number of terms is called the length of the _____. Unlike a set, order matters, and the exact same elements can appear multiple times at different positions in the _____.
- a. Thing
- b. Sequence0
- c. Undefined
- d. Undefined

131. Elementary _____ are simple transformations which can be applied to a matrix without changing the linear system of equations that it represents.

Chapter 6. Systems of Equations and Inequalities

    a. Thing
    c. Undefined
    b. Row operations0
    d. Undefined

132. _____ is the study of algorithms for the problems of continuous mathematics as distinguished from discrete mathematics.
    a. Thing
    c. Undefined
    b. Numerical analysis0
    d. Undefined

133. The _____, in practice often shortened to amp, is a unit of electric current, or amount of electric charge per second.
    a. Amperes0
    c. Undefined
    b. Thing
    d. Undefined

134. _____ is the level of functional and/or metabolic efficiency of an organism at both the micro level.
    a. Health0
    c. Undefined
    b. Thing
    d. Undefined

135. In sociology and biology a _____ is the collection of people or organisms of a particular species living in a given geographic area or space, usually measured by a census.
    a. Population0
    c. Undefined
    b. Thing
    d. Undefined

136. _____ is the process of recording pictures by means of capturing light on a light-sensitive medium, such as a film or sensor.
    a. Thing
    c. Undefined
    b. Photography0
    d. Undefined

137. In linear algebra, real numbers are called scalars and relate to vectors in a vector space through the operation of _____ multiplication, in which a vector can be multiplied by a number to produce another vector.
    a. Thing
    c. Undefined
    b. Scalar0
    d. Undefined

138. In Euclidean geometry, a uniform _____ is a linear transformation that enlargers or diminishes objects, and whose _____ factor is the same in all directions. This is also called homothethy.
    a. Thing
    c. Undefined
    b. Scale0
    d. Undefined

139. In mathematics, a _____ is an algebraic structure in which addition and multiplication are defined and have properties listed below.
    a. Ring0
    c. Undefined
    b. Thing
    d. Undefined

140. In geographic information systems, a _____ comprises an entity with a geographic location, typically determined by points, arcs, or polygons. Carriageways and cadastres exemplify _____ data.

Chapter 6. Systems of Equations and Inequalities

    a. Thing
    b. Feature0
    c. Undefined
    d. Undefined

141. The _____ is a property of multiplication or addition where the product or sum remains the same, regardless of whether or not the order of the addends or factors are changed.
    a. Commutative property0
    b. Thing
    c. Undefined
    d. Undefined

142. In mathematics, defined and _____ are used to explain whether or not expressions have meaningful, sensible, and unambiguous values.
    a. Thing
    b. Undefined0
    c. Undefined
    d. Undefined

143. In mathematics, a _____ is the result of multiplying, or an expression that identifies factors to be multiplied.
    a. Product0
    b. Thing
    c. Undefined
    d. Undefined

144. _____ is one of the basic operations defining a vector space in linear algebra.
    a. Thing
    b. Scalar multiplication0
    c. Undefined
    d. Undefined

145. In mathematics, and in particular in abstract algebra, the _____ is a property of binary operations that generalises the distributive law from elementary algebra.
    a. Distributive property0
    b. Thing
    c. Undefined
    d. Undefined

146. In statistics, a _____ measure is one which is measuring what is supposed to measure.
    a. Valid0
    b. Thing
    c. Undefined
    d. Undefined

147. In mathematics, _____ is a property that a binary operation can have. Within an expression containing two or more of the same associative operators in a row, the order of operations does not matter as long as the sequence of the operands is not changed.
    a. Associativity0
    b. Thing
    c. Undefined
    d. Undefined

148. In mathematics, _____ is a part of the set theoretic notion of function.
    a. Thing
    b. Image0
    c. Undefined
    d. Undefined

149. In mathematics, a _____ of a positive integer n is a way of writing n as a sum of positive integers.
    a. Thing
    b. Composition0
    c. Undefined
    d. Undefined

150. _____ element of an element x with respect to a binary operation * with identity element e is an element y such that $x * y = y * x = e$. In particular,

a. Inverse0 b. Thing
c. Undefined d. Undefined

151. An _____ is a function which does the reverse of a given function.
   a. Inverse function0 b. Thing
   c. Undefined d. Undefined

152. In mathematics, the idea of _____ generalises the concepts of negation, in relation to addition, and reciprocal, in relation to multiplication.
   a. Inverse element0 b. Thing
   c. Undefined d. Undefined

153. In mathematics, a _____ in elementary terms is any of a variety of different functions from geometry, such as rotations, reflections and translations.
   a. Transformation0 b. Thing
   c. Undefined d. Undefined

154. In Euclidean geometry, a _____ is moving every point a constant distance in a specified direction.
   a. Concept b. Translation0
   c. Undefined d. Undefined

155. A _____ is a statement or claimt that a particular event will occur in the future in more certain terms than a forecast.
   a. Prediction0 b. Thing
   c. Undefined d. Undefined

156. A _____ is a movement of an object in a circular motion. A two-dimensional object rotates around a center (or point) of _____. A three-dimensional object rotates around a line called an axis. If the axis of _____ is within the body, the body is said to rotate upon itself, or spin—which implies relative speed and perhaps free-movement with angular momentum. A circular motion about an external point, e.g. the Earth about the Sun, is called an orbit or more properly an orbital revolution.
   a. Rotation0 b. Thing
   c. Undefined d. Undefined

157. In algebra, a _____ is a function depending on n that associates a scalar, $det(A)$, to every $n \times n$ square matrix A.
   a. Determinant0 b. Thing
   c. Undefined d. Undefined

158. A _____ is a deliberate process for transforming one or more inputs into one or more results.
   a. Calculation0 b. Thing
   c. Undefined d. Undefined

159. In linear algebra, a _____ or minor of a matrix A is the determinant of some smaller square matrix, cut down from A.

a. Cofactor0
b. Thing
c. Undefined
d. Undefined

160. An _____ is a square matrix which has an inverse.
   a. Invertible matrix0
   b. Thing
   c. Undefined
   d. Undefined

161. In linear algebra, a _____ of a matrix A is the determinant of some smaller square matrix, cut down from A.
   a. Thing
   b. Minor0
   c. Undefined
   d. Undefined

162. A _____ is a four-sided plane figure that has two sets of opposite parallel sides.
   a. Parallelogram0
   b. Concept
   c. Undefined
   d. Undefined

163. In geometry, two sets are called _____ if one can be transformed into the other by an isometry, i.e., a combination of translations, rotations and reflections.
   a. Congruent0
   b. Thing
   c. Undefined
   d. Undefined

164. Three or more points that lie on the same line are called _____.
   a. Collinear0
   b. Thing
   c. Undefined
   d. Undefined

165. In Euclidean geometry, an _____ is a closed segment of a differentiable curve in the two-dimensional plane; for example, a circular _____ is a segment of a circle.
   a. Concept
   b. Arc0
   c. Undefined
   d. Undefined

166. In mathematics, an inequality is a statement about the relative size or order of two objects. For example 14 > 10, or 14 is _____ 10.
   a. Thing
   b. Greater than0
   c. Undefined
   d. Undefined

167. In mathematical logic, a Gödel numbering (or Gödel _____) is a function that assigns to each symbol and well-formed formula of some formal language a unique natural number called its Gödel number.
   a. Thing
   b. Code0
   c. Undefined
   d. Undefined

168. In geometry, a line _____ is a part of a line that is bounded by two end points, and contains every point on the line between its end points.
   a. Segment0
   b. Concept
   c. Undefined
   d. Undefined

169. Mathematical _____ is used to represent ideas.

Chapter 6. Systems of Equations and Inequalities

    a. Notation0
    b. Thing
    c. Undefined
    d. Undefined

170. In mathematics, the _____ of a function is the set of all "output" values produced by that function. Given a function $f : A \to B$, the _____ of f, is defined to be the set $\{x \in B : x = f(a) \text{ for some } a \in A\}$.
    a. Range0
    b. Thing
    c. Undefined
    d. Undefined

171. A _____ is a part of a line that is bounded by two end points, and contains every point on the line between its end points.
    a. Thing
    b. Line segment0
    c. Undefined
    d. Undefined

172. In elementary algebra, an _____ is a set that contains every real number between two indicated numbers and may contain the two numbers themselves.
    a. Interval0
    b. Thing
    c. Undefined
    d. Undefined

173. _____ is the notation in which permitted values for a variable are expressed as ranging over a certain interval; "5 < x < 9" is an example of the application of _____.
    a. Interval notation0
    b. Thing
    c. Undefined
    d. Undefined

174. _____ is the middle point of a line segment.
    a. Thing
    b. Midpoint0
    c. Undefined
    d. Undefined

175. In mathematics, a _____ of a k-place relation $L \subseteq X_1 \times \ldots \times X_k$ is one of the sets X_j, $1 \leq j \leq k$. In the special case where k = 2 and $L \subseteq X_1 \times X_2$ is a function $L : X_1 \to X_2$, it is conventional to refer to X_1 as the _____ of the function and to refer to X_2 as the codomain of the function.
    a. Domain0
    b. Thing
    c. Undefined
    d. Undefined

176. A _____ is a first degree polynomial mathematical function of the form: $f(x) = mx + b$ where m and b are real constants and x is a real variable.
    a. Linear function0
    b. Thing
    c. Undefined
    d. Undefined

177. _____ is often used to describe the measurement of the steepness, incline, gradient, or grade of a straight line. The _____ is defined as the ratio of the "rise" divided by the "run" between two points on a line, or in other words, the ratio of the altitude change to the horizontal distance between any two points on the line.
    a. Thing
    b. Slope0
    c. Undefined
    d. Undefined

178. In mathematics, a _____ is the end result of a division problem. It can also be expressed as the number of times the divisor divides into the dividend.

a. Quotient0
b. Thing
c. Undefined
d. Undefined

179. The function difference divided by the point difference is known as the _____
    a. Thing
    b. Difference quotient0
    c. Undefined
    d. Undefined

180. A _____ function is a function for which, intuitively, small changes in the input result in small changes in the output.
    a. Event
    b. Continuous0
    c. Undefined
    d. Undefined

181. _____ of a polynomial with real or complex coefficients is a certain expression in the coefficients of the polynomial which is equal to zero if and only if the polynomial has a multiple root i.e. a root with multiplicity greater than one in the complex numbers.
    a. Thing
    b. Discriminant0
    c. Undefined
    d. Undefined

182. _____ is a technique used in algebra to solve quadratic equations, in analytic geometry for determining the shapes of graphs, and in calculus for computing integrals, including, but hardly limited to, the integrals that define Laplace transforms. The essential objective is to reduce a quadratic polynomial in a variable in an equation or expression to a squared polynomial of linear order. This can reduce an equation or integral to one that is more easily solved or evaluated.
    a. Completing the square0
    b. Thing
    c. Undefined
    d. Undefined

183. _____ is a function of the form
    a. Thing
    b. Cubic function0
    c. Undefined
    d. Undefined

184. in mathematics, maxima and minima, known collectively as _____, are the largest value maximum or smallest value minimum, that a function takes in a point either within a given neighborhood or on the function domain in its entirety global extremum.
    a. Thing
    b. Extrema0
    c. Undefined
    d. Undefined

185. A real-valued function f defined on the real line is said to have a _____ point at the point $x*$, if there exists some $\varepsilon > 0$, such that f when $x - x* < \varepsilon$.
    a. Local maximum0
    b. Thing
    c. Undefined
    d. Undefined

186. The _____ of a member of a multiset is how many memberships in the multiset it has.
    a. Multiplicity0
    b. Thing
    c. Undefined
    d. Undefined

187. In mathematics, there are several meanings of _____ depending on the subject.

Chapter 6. Systems of Equations and Inequalities

    a. Degree0
    c. Undefined
    b. Thing
    d. Undefined

188. In mathematics, a _____ is an expression that is constructed from one or more variables and constants, using only the operations of addition, subtraction, multiplication, and constant positive whole number exponents. is a _____. Note in particular that division by an expression containing a variable is not in general allowed in polynomials. [1]
    a. Polynomial0
    c. Undefined
    b. Thing
    d. Undefined

189. In mathematics and elsewhere, the adjective _____ means fourth order, such as the function x4. A _____ number is a number which equals the fourth power of an integer.
    a. Thing
    c. Undefined
    b. Quartic0
    d. Undefined

190. _____ is a notation for writing numbers that is often used by scientists and mathematicians to make it easier to write large and small numbers.
    a. Scientific notation0
    c. Undefined
    b. Thing
    d. Undefined

191. An _____ is a straight line or curve A to which another curve B approaches closer and closer as one moves along it. As one moves along B, the space between it and the _____ A becomes smaller and smaller, and can in fact be made as small as one could wish by going far enough along. A curve may or may not touch or cross its _____. In fact, the curve may intersect the _____ an infinite number of times.
    a. Thing
    c. Undefined
    b. Asymptote0
    d. Undefined

192. In astronomy, geography, geometry and related sciences and contexts, a plane is said to be _____ at a given point if it is locally perpendicular to the gradient of the gravity field, i.e., with the direction of the gravitational force at that point.
    a. Thing
    c. Undefined
    b. Horizontal0
    d. Undefined

193. _____ is the symbold used to indicate the nth root of a number
    a. Radical0
    c. Undefined
    b. Thing
    d. Undefined

194. In mathematics, a _____ is the set of all points in three-dimensional space (R^3) which are at distance r from a fixed point of that space, where r is a positive real number called the radius of the _____. The fixed point is called the center or centre, and is not part of the _____ itself.
    a. Thing
    c. Undefined
    b. Sphere0
    d. Undefined

195. _____ is a temperature scale named after the German physicist Daniel Gabriel _____ , who proposed it in 1724.
    a. Fahrenheit0
    c. Undefined
    b. Thing
    d. Undefined

Chapter 6. Systems of Equations and Inequalities

196. _____ is, or relates to, the _____ temperature scale .
   a. Thing   b. Celsius0
   c. Undefined   d. Undefined

197. _____ is the process in which two clone daughter cells are produced by the cell division of one bacterium.
   a. Bacteria growth0   b. Thing
   c. Undefined   d. Undefined

198. In mathematics, a _____ section is a curve that can be formed by intersecting a cone with a plane.
   a. Thing   b. Conic0
   c. Undefined   d. Undefined

199. The _____ is defined as the summation of all particles and energy that exist and the space-time which all events occur.
   a. Thing   b. Universe0
   c. Undefined   d. Undefined

200. _____ of Perga was a Greek geometer and astronomer, of the Alexandrian school, noted for his writings on conic sections. His innovative methodology and terminology, especially in the field of conics, influenced many later scholars including Ptolemy, Francesco Maurolico, Isaac Newton, and René Descartes. It was _____ who gave the ellipse, the parabola, and the hyperbola the names by which we know them. The hypothesis of eccentric orbits, or equivalently, deferent and epicycles, to explain the apparent motion of the planets and the varying speed of the Moon, are also attributed to him.
   a. Person   b. Apollonius0
   c. Undefined   d. Undefined

201. _____, born Tyge Ottesen Brahe was a Danish nobleman from the region of Scania in moder day Sweden. He is best known today as an early astronomer, though in his lifetime he was also well known as an astrologer and alchemist.
   a. Tycho Brahe0   b. Person
   c. Undefined   d. Undefined

202. _____ was a German Lutheran mathematician, astronomer and astrologer, and a key figure in the 17th century astronomical revolution.
   a. Person   b. Johannes Kepler0
   c. Undefined   d. Undefined

203. In physics, an _____ is the path that an object makes around another object while under the influence of a source of centripetal force, such as gravity.
   a. Thing   b. Orbit0
   c. Undefined   d. Undefined

204. A _____, as defined by the International Astronomical Union , is a celestial body orbiting a star or stellar remnant that is massive enough to be rounded by its own gravity, not massive enough to cause thermonuclear fusion in its core, and has cleared its neighboring region of planetesimals.
   a. Thing   b. Planet0
   c. Undefined   d. Undefined

Chapter 6. Systems of Equations and Inequalities

205. Sir Isaac _____, was an English physicist, mathematician, astronomer, natural philosopher, and alchemist, regarded by many as the greatest figure in the history of science
   a. Person
   b. Newton0
   c. Undefined
   d. Undefined

206. _____ is the state of being greater than any finite real or natural number, however large.
   a. Thing
   b. Infinite0
   c. Undefined
   d. Undefined

207. In mathematics, an _____ .
   a. Thing
   b. Ellipse0
   c. Undefined
   d. Undefined

208. In mathematics, a _____ is a type of conic section defined as the intersection between a right circular conical surface and a plane which cuts through both halves of the cone.
   a. Hyperbola0
   b. Thing
   c. Undefined
   d. Undefined

Chapter 7. Conic Sections

1. In mathematics, the _____ is a conic section generated by the intersection of a right circular conical surface and a plane parallel to a generating straight line of that surface. It can also be defined as locus of points in a plane which are equidistant from a given point.
   - a. Thing
   - b. Parabola0
   - c. Undefined
   - d. Undefined

2. In mathematics, a _____ is a two-dimensional manifold or surface that is perfectly flat.
   - a. Plane0
   - b. Thing
   - c. Undefined
   - d. Undefined

3. A _____ is a three-dimensional geometric shape formed by straight lines through a fixed point (vertex) to the points of a fixed curve (directrix)
   - a. Concept
   - b. Cone0
   - c. Undefined
   - d. Undefined

4. In mathematics, a _____ section is a curve that can be formed by intersecting a cone with a plane.
   - a. Conic0
   - b. Thing
   - c. Undefined
   - d. Undefined

5. In mathematics, an _____ .
   - a. Thing
   - b. Ellipse0
   - c. Undefined
   - d. Undefined

6. In mathematics, a _____ is a type of conic section defined as the intersection between a right circular conical surface and a plane which cuts through both halves of the cone.
   - a. Thing
   - b. Hyperbola0
   - c. Undefined
   - d. Undefined

7. _____ is a test to determine if a relation or its graph is a function or not
   - a. Thing
   - b. Vertical line test0
   - c. Undefined
   - d. Undefined

8. Acid _____ ratio measures the ability of a company to use its near cash or quick assets to immediately extinguish its current liabilities.
   - a. Test0
   - b. Thing
   - c. Undefined
   - d. Undefined

9. The mathematical concept of a _____ expresses the intuitive idea of deterministic dependence between two quantities, one of which is viewed as primary and the other as secondary. A _____ then is a way to associate a unique output for each input of a specified type, for example, a real number or an element of a given set.
   - a. Function0
   - b. Thing
   - c. Undefined
   - d. Undefined

10. A _____ is a symbolic representation denoting a quantity or expression. It often represents an "unknown" quantity that has the potential to change.

Chapter 7. Conic Sections

   a. Thing
   b. Variable0
   c. Undefined
   d. Undefined

11. In geometry, a _____ is a special kind of point, usually a corner of a polygon, polyhedron, or higher dimensional polytope. In the geometry of curves a _____ is a point of where the first derivative of curvature is zero. In graph theory, a _____ is the fundamental unit out of which graphs are formed
   a. Thing
   b. Vertex0
   c. Undefined
   d. Undefined

12. An _____ is a straight line around which a geometric figure can be rotated.
   a. Axis0
   b. Thing
   c. Undefined
   d. Undefined

13. In astronomy, geography, geometry and related sciences and contexts, a plane is said to be _____ at a given point if it is locally perpendicular to the gradient of the gravity field, i.e., with the direction of the gravitational force at that point.
   a. Thing
   b. Horizontal0
   c. Undefined
   d. Undefined

14. _____ are the basic objects of study in graph theory. Informally speaking, a graph is a set of objects called points, nodes, or vertices connected by links called lines or edges.
   a. Graphs0
   b. Thing
   c. Undefined
   d. Undefined

15. A _____ given two distinct points A and B on the _____, is the set of points C on the line containing points A and B such that A is not strictly between C and B.
   a. Ray0
   b. Thing
   c. Undefined
   d. Undefined

16. In geometry and physics, _____ are half-lines that continue forever in one direction.
   a. Rays0
   b. Thing
   c. Undefined
   d. Undefined

17. In _____ algebra, a *-ring is an associative ring with an antilinear, antiautomorphism * : A ¨ A which is an involution.
   a. Star0
   b. Thing
   c. Undefined
   d. Undefined

18. _____ is a quadric
   a. Thing
   b. Paraboloid0
   c. Undefined
   d. Undefined

19. _____ is electromagnetic radiation with a wavelength that is visible to the eye (visible _____) or, in a technical or scientific context, electromagnetic radiation of any wavelength.
   a. Thing
   b. Light0
   c. Undefined
   d. Undefined

Chapter 7. Conic Sections

20. _____ is a set, with some particular properties and usually some additional structure, such as the operations of addition or multiplication, for instance.
    a. Thing
    b. Space0
    c. Undefined
    d. Undefined

21. In geometry, a _____ (Greek words diairo = divide and metro = measure) of a circle is any straight line segment that passes through the centre and whose endpoints are on the circular boundary, or, in more modern usage, the length of such a line segment. When using the word in the more modern sense, one speaks of the _____ rather than a _____, because all diameters of a circle have the same length. This length is twice the radius. The _____ of a circle is also the longest chord that the circle has.
    a. Diameter0
    b. Thing
    c. Undefined
    d. Undefined

22. In geometry, a _____ is the intersection of a body in 2-dimensional space with a line, or of a body in 3-dimensional space with a plane
    a. Thing
    b. Cross section0
    c. Undefined
    d. Undefined

23. The _____ of measurement are a globally standardized and modernized form of the metric system.
    a. Units0
    b. Thing
    c. Undefined
    d. Undefined

24. A _____ is a set of numbers that designate location in a given reference system, such as x,y in a planar _____ system or an x,y,z in a three-dimensional _____ system.
    a. Thing
    b. Coordinate0
    c. Undefined
    d. Undefined

25. In plane geometry, a _____ is a polygon with four equal sides, four right angles, and parallel opposite sides. In algebra, the _____ of a number is that number multiplied by itself.
    a. Thing
    b. Square0
    c. Undefined
    d. Undefined

26. _____ is a technique used in algebra to solve quadratic equations, in analytic geometry for determining the shapes of graphs, and in calculus for computing integrals, including, but hardly limited to, the integrals that define Laplace transforms. The essential objective is to reduce a quadratic polynomial in a variable in an equation or expression to a squared polynomial of linear order. This can reduce an equation or integral to one that is more easily solved or evaluated.
    a. Completing the square0
    b. Thing
    c. Undefined
    d. Undefined

27. Equivalence is the condition of being _____ or essentially equal.
    a. Equivalent0
    b. Thing
    c. Undefined
    d. Undefined

28. A _____ is a polynomial consisting of three terms; in other words, it is the sum of three monomials.

a. Trinomial0
b. Thing
c. Undefined
d. Undefined

29. The term _____ can refer to an integer which is the square of some other integer, or an algebraic expression that can be factored as the square of some other expression.
   a. Perfect square0
   b. Thing
   c. Undefined
   d. Undefined

30. _____ is a branch of mathematics concerning the study of structure, relation and quantity.
   a. Concept
   b. Algebra0
   c. Undefined
   d. Undefined

31. In classical geometry, a _____ of a circle or sphere is any line segment from its center to its boundary. By extension, the _____ of a circle or sphere is the length of any such segment. The _____ is half the diameter. In science and engineering the term _____ of curvature is commonly used as a synonym for _____.
   a. Radius0
   b. Thing
   c. Undefined
   d. Undefined

32. _____ is the transport of people on a trip/journey or the process or time involved in a person or object moving from one location to another.
   a. Travel0
   b. Thing
   c. Undefined
   d. Undefined

33. In mathematics and the mathematical sciences, a _____ is a fixed, but possibly unspecified, value. This is in contrast to a variable, which is not fixed.
   a. Thing
   b. Constant0
   c. Undefined
   d. Undefined

34. In physics, an _____ is the path that an object makes around another object while under the influence of a source of centripetal force, such as gravity.
   a. Orbit0
   b. Thing
   c. Undefined
   d. Undefined

35. A _____, as defined by the International Astronomical Union, is a celestial body orbiting a star or stellar remnant that is massive enough to be rounded by its own gravity, not massive enough to cause thermonuclear fusion in its core, and has cleared its neighboring region of planetesimals.
   a. Thing
   b. Planet0
   c. Undefined
   d. Undefined

36. A _____ is a statement or claimt that a particular event will occur in the future in more certain terms than a forecast.
   a. Thing
   b. Prediction0
   c. Undefined
   d. Undefined

37. Compass and straightedge or ruler-and-compass _____ is the _____ of lengths or angles using only an idealized ruler and compass.

Chapter 7. Conic Sections

    a. Construction0
    c. Undefined
    b. Thing
    d. Undefined

38. In mathematics, the concept of a _____ tries to capture the intuitive idea of a geometrical one-dimensional and continuous object. A simple example is the circle.
    a. Curve0
    c. Undefined
    b. Thing
    d. Undefined

39. A _____ is the result of the addition of a set of numbers. The numbers may be natural numbers, complex numbers, matrices, or still more complicated objects. An infinite _____ is a subtle procedure known as a series.
    a. Thing
    c. Undefined
    b. Sum0
    d. Undefined

40. In geometry, the _____ are a pair of special points used in describing conic sections. The four types of conic sections are the circle, parabola, ellipse, and hyperbola.
    a. Foci0
    c. Undefined
    b. Thing
    d. Undefined

41. In Euclidean geometry, a _____ is the set of all points in a plane at a fixed distance, called the radius, from a given point, the center.
    a. Circle0
    c. Undefined
    b. Thing
    d. Undefined

42. In geometry, a line _____ is a part of a line that is bounded by two end points, and contains every point on the line between its end points.
    a. Concept
    c. Undefined
    b. Segment0
    d. Undefined

43. A _____ is a part of a line that is bounded by two end points, and contains every point on the line between its end points.
    a. Line segment0
    c. Undefined
    b. Thing
    d. Undefined

44. In linear algebra, a _____ of a matrix A is the determinant of some smaller square matrix, cut down from A.
    a. Thing
    c. Undefined
    b. Minor0
    d. Undefined

45. In geometry, an _____ is a point at which a line segment or ray terminates.
    a. Endpoint0
    c. Undefined
    b. Thing
    d. Undefined

46. In geometry, the _____ of an object is a point in some sense in the middle of the object.
    a. Center0
    c. Undefined
    b. Thing
    d. Undefined

47. An _____ is when two lines intersect somewhere on a plane creating a right angle at intersection

a. Thing
b. Axes0
c. Undefined
d. Undefined

48. _____ is a notation for writing numbers that is often used by scientists and mathematicians to make it easier to write large and small numbers.
   a. Thing
   b. Scientific notation0
   c. Undefined
   d. Undefined

49. _____ is a parameter associated with every conic section.
   a. Thing
   b. Eccentricity0
   c. Undefined
   d. Undefined

50. In mathematics, _____ growth occurs when the growth rate of a function is always proportional to the function's current size.
   a. Exponential0
   b. Thing
   c. Undefined
   d. Undefined

51. _____ is one of the most important functions in mathematics. A function commonly used to study growth and decay
   a. Exponential function0
   b. Thing
   c. Undefined
   d. Undefined

52. In mathematics, an _____ number is any real number that is not a rational number- that is, it is a number which cannot be expressed as a fraction m/n, where m and n are integers.
   a. Thing
   b. Irrational0
   c. Undefined
   d. Undefined

53. In mathematics, an _____ is any real number that is not a rational number ¡ª that is, it is a number which cannot be expressed as m/n, where m and n are integers.
   a. Irrational number0
   b. Thing
   c. Undefined
   d. Undefined

54. In Euclidean geometry, a _____ is moving every point a constant distance in a specified direction.
   a. Translation0
   b. Concept
   c. Undefined
   d. Undefined

55. In geometry, two sets are called _____ if one can be transformed into the other by an isometry, i.e., a combination of translations, rotations and reflections.
   a. Congruent0
   b. Thing
   c. Undefined
   d. Undefined

56. _____ systems represent systems whose behavior is not expressible as a sum of the behaviors of its descriptors.
   a. Thing
   b. Nonlinear0
   c. Undefined
   d. Undefined

Chapter 7. Conic Sections

57. _____ are a set of equations containing multiple variables.
   a. Thing
   b. Systems of equations0
   c. Undefined
   d. Undefined

58. In mathematics, an _____ is a statement about the relative size or order of two objects.
   a. Thing
   b. Inequality0
   c. Undefined
   d. Undefined

59. In mathematics, a _____ of a complex-valued function f is a member x of the domain of f such that f(x) vanishes at x, that is, x : f (x) = 0.
   a. Root0
   b. Thing
   c. Undefined
   d. Undefined

60. A _____ is a set of possible values that a variable can take on in order to satisfy a given set of conditions, which may include equations and inequalities.
   a. Solution set0
   b. Thing
   c. Undefined
   d. Undefined

61. In mathematics, the _____ of a coordinate system is the point where the axes of the system intersect.
   a. Origin0
   b. Thing
   c. Undefined
   d. Undefined

62. The _____ (symbol _____) and the millibar (symbol mbar, also mb) are units of pressure.
   a. Thing
   b. Bar0
   c. Undefined
   d. Undefined

63. An _____ is a type of quadric surface that is a higher dimensional analogue of an ellipse.
   a. Thing
   b. Ellipsoid0
   c. Undefined
   d. Undefined

64. A _____ is a unit of length, usually used to measure distance, in a number of different systems, including Imperial units, United States customary units and Norwegian/Swedish mil. Its size can vary from system to system, but in each is between 1 and 10 kilometers. In contemporary English contexts _____ refers to either:
   a. Mile0
   b. Thing
   c. Undefined
   d. Undefined

65. _____ of an object is its speed in a particular direction.
   a. Thing
   b. Velocity0
   c. Undefined
   d. Undefined

66. A _____ is a unit of length in the metric system, equal to one thousand metres, the current SI base unit of length
   a. Thing
   b. Kilometer0
   c. Undefined
   d. Undefined

Chapter 7. Conic Sections

67. _____ is the distance around a given two-dimensional object. As a general rule, the _____ of a polygon can always be calculated by adding all the length of the sides together. So, the formula for triangles is P = a + b + c, where a, b and c stand for each side of it. For quadrilaterals the equation is P = a + b + c + d. For equilateral polygons, P = na, where n is the number of sides and a is the side length.
   a. Perimeter0
   b. Thing
   c. Undefined
   d. Undefined

68. In business, particularly accounting, a _____ is the time intervals that the accounts, statement, payments, or other calculations cover.
   a. Period0
   b. Thing
   c. Undefined
   d. Undefined

69. A _____, known as a parabolic dish or a parabolic mirror, is a reflective device, commonly formed in the shape of a paraboloid of revolution.
   a. Parabolic reflector0
   b. Thing
   c. Undefined
   d. Undefined

70. In algebra, a _____ is a binomial formed by taking the opposite of the second term of a binomial.
   a. Conjugate0
   b. Thing
   c. Undefined
   d. Undefined

71. An _____ is a straight line or curve A to which another curve B approaches closer and closer as one moves along it. As one moves along B, the space between it and the _____ A becomes smaller and smaller, and can in fact be made as small as one could wish by going far enough along. A curve may or may not touch or cross its _____. In fact, the curve may intersect the _____ an infinite number of times.
   a. Thing
   b. Asymptote0
   c. Undefined
   d. Undefined

72. In geometry, a _____ is defined as a quadrilateral where all four of its angles are right angles.
   a. Rectangle0
   b. Thing
   c. Undefined
   d. Undefined

73. In mathematics, _____ geometry was the traditional name for the geometry of three-dimensional Euclidean space — for practical purposes the kind of space we live in.
   a. Thing
   b. Solid0
   c. Undefined
   d. Undefined

74. In mathematics, _____ are the intuitive idea of a geometrical one-dimensional and continuous object.
   a. Thing
   b. Curves0
   c. Undefined
   d. Undefined

75. _____ is the path a moving object follows through space.
   a. Thing
   b. Projectile motion0
   c. Undefined
   d. Undefined

Chapter 7. Conic Sections

76. _____, in economics and political economy, are the distributions or payments awarded to the various suppliers of the factors of production.
    a. Returns0
    b. Thing
    c. Undefined
    d. Undefined

77. A _____ can refer to a line joining two nonadjacent vertices of a polygon or polyhedron, or in some contexts any upward or downward sloping line. .
    a. Thing
    b. Diagonal0
    c. Undefined
    d. Undefined

78. In mathematics, the _____ of two sets A and B is the set that contains all elements of A that also belong to B (or equivalently, all elements of B that also belong to A), but no other elements.
    a. Thing
    b. Intersection0
    c. Undefined
    d. Undefined

79. In linear algebra, the _____ of an n-by-n square matrix A is defined to be the sum of the elements on the main diagonal of A,
    a. Trace0
    b. Thing
    c. Undefined
    d. Undefined

80. The metre (or _____, see spelling differences) is a measure of length. It is the basic unit of length in the metric system and in the International System of Units (SI), used around the world for general and scientific purposes.
    a. Meter0
    b. Concept
    c. Undefined
    d. Undefined

81. _____, Greek for "knowledge of nature," is the branch of science concerned with the discovery and characterization of universal laws which govern matter, energy, space, and time.
    a. Thing
    b. Physics0
    c. Undefined
    d. Undefined

82. In mathematics, an inequality is a statement about the relative size or order of two objects. For example 14 > 10, or 14 is _____ 10.
    a. Greater than0
    b. Thing
    c. Undefined
    d. Undefined

83. In mathematics, an _____, mean, or central tendency of a data set refers to a measure of the "middle" or "expected" value of the data set.
    a. Concept
    b. Average0
    c. Undefined
    d. Undefined

84. _____ was a German mathematician. he is best known as the creator of set theory. He Cantor established the importance of one-to-one correspondence between sets, defined infinite and well–ordered sets, and proved that the real numbers are "more numerous" than the natural numbers.
    a. Thing
    b. Georg Cantor0
    c. Undefined
    d. Undefined

Chapter 7. Conic Sections

85. _____ or arithmetics is the oldest and most elementary branch of mathematics, used by almost everyone, for tasks ranging from simple daily counting to advanced science and business calculations.
   a. Thing
   b. Arithmetic0
   c. Undefined
   d. Undefined

86. A _____ is a deliberate process for transforming one or more inputs into one or more results.
   a. Thing
   b. Calculation0
   c. Undefined
   d. Undefined

87. In business, _____ are commonly referred to as _____ assets or intellectual capital.
   a. Thing
   b. Intangible0
   c. Undefined
   d. Undefined

88. _____ is the process of recording pictures by means of capturing light on a light-sensitive medium, such as a film or sensor.
   a. Photography0
   b. Thing
   c. Undefined
   d. Undefined

Chapter 8. Further Topics in Algebra

1. In mathematics, a _____ is an ordered list of objects. Like a set, it contains members, also called elements or terms, and the number of terms is called the length of the _____. Unlike a set, order matters, and the exact same elements can appear multiple times at different positions in the _____.
   a. Thing
   b. Sequence0
   c. Undefined
   d. Undefined

2. The mathematical concept of a _____ expresses the intuitive idea of deterministic dependence between two quantities, one of which is viewed as primary and the other as secondary. A _____ then is a way to associate a unique output for each input of a specified type, for example, a real number or an element of a given set.
   a. Function0
   b. Thing
   c. Undefined
   d. Undefined

3. U.S. liquid _____ is legally defined as 231 cubic inches, and is equal to 3.785411784 litres or abotu 0.13368 cubic feet. This is the most common definition of a _____. The U.S. fluid ounce is defined as 1/128 of a U.S. _____.
   a. Thing
   b. Gallon0
   c. Undefined
   d. Undefined

4. _____ is the fee paid on borrowed money.
   a. Thing
   b. Interest0
   c. Undefined
   d. Undefined

5. A _____ are accounts maintained by commercial banks, savings and loan associations, credit unions, and mutual savings banks that pay interest but can not be used directly as money by, for example, writing a cheque.
   a. Thing
   b. Savings account0
   c. Undefined
   d. Undefined

6. In banking and accountancy, the outstanding _____ is the amount of money owned, or due, that remains in a deposit account or a loan account at a given date, after all past remittances, payments and withdrawal have been accounted for.
   a. Balance0
   b. Thing
   c. Undefined
   d. Undefined

7. In mathematics, a _____ can mean either an element of the set {1, 2, 3, ...} (i.e the positive integers or the counting numbers) or an element of the set {0, 1, 2, 3, ...} (i.e. the non-negative integers).
   a. Natural number0
   b. Thing
   c. Undefined
   d. Undefined

8. _____ is the state of being greater than any finite real or natural number, however large.
   a. Infinite0
   b. Thing
   c. Undefined
   d. Undefined

9. In mathematics, a _____ of a k-place relation $L \subseteq X_1 \times ... \times X_k$ is one of the sets X_j, $1 \leq j \leq k$. In the special case where k = 2 and $L \subseteq X_1 \times X_2$ is a function $L : X_1 \to X_2$, it is conventional to refer to X_1 as the _____ of the function and to refer to X_2 as the codomain of the function.
   a. Thing
   b. Domain0
   c. Undefined
   d. Undefined

10. In mathematics, a set is called _____ if there is a bijection between the set and some set of the form {1, 2, ..., n} where n is a natural number.
   a. Finite0
   b. Thing
   c. Undefined
   d. Undefined

11. In statistics, _____ means the most frequent value assumed by a random variable, or occurring in a sampling of a random variable.
   a. Concept
   b. Mode0
   c. Undefined
   d. Undefined

12. In mathematics, an _____, mean, or central tendency of a data set refers to a measure of the "middle" or "expected" value of the data set.
   a. Concept
   b. Average0
   c. Undefined
   d. Undefined

13. A _____, as defined by the International Astronomical Union, is a celestial body orbiting a star or stellar remnant that is massive enough to be rounded by its own gravity, not massive enough to cause thermonuclear fusion in its core, and has cleared its neighboring region of planetesimals.
   a. Planet0
   b. Thing
   c. Undefined
   d. Undefined

14. An _____, also called a minor planet or planetoid, comes from a class of atsronomical objects.
   a. Asteroid0
   b. Thing
   c. Undefined
   d. Undefined

15. In mathematics, when a method of defining functions is utilized, in which the function being defined is applied within its own definition, that pertaining function is called _____.
   a. Thing
   b. Recursive0
   c. Undefined
   d. Undefined

16. In sociology and biology a _____ is the collection of people or organisms of a particular species living in a given geographic area or space, usually measured by a census.
   a. Population0
   b. Thing
   c. Undefined
   d. Undefined

17. Mathematical _____ are the wide variety of ways to capture an abstract mathematical concept or relationship.
   a. Representations0
   b. Thing
   c. Undefined
   d. Undefined

18. _____ is mass m per unit volume V.
   a. Thing
   b. Density0
   c. Undefined
   d. Undefined

19. _____ is a form of periodic payment from an employer to an employee, which is specified in an employment contract.

a. Gross pay0
b. Thing
c. Undefined
d. Undefined

20. The word _____ comes from the Latin word linearis, which means created by lines.
    a. Linear0
    b. Thing
    c. Undefined
    d. Undefined

21. A _____ is a first degree polynomial mathematical function of the form: f(x) = mx + b where m and b are real constants and x is a real variable.
    a. Linear function0
    b. Thing
    c. Undefined
    d. Undefined

22. A _____ is a form of periodic payment from an employer to an employee, which is specified in an employment contract.
    a. Thing
    b. Salary0
    c. Undefined
    d. Undefined

23. _____ or arithmetics is the oldest and most elementary branch of mathematics, used by almost everyone, for tasks ranging from simple daily counting to advanced science and business calculations.
    a. Thing
    b. Arithmetic0
    c. Undefined
    d. Undefined

24. _____ is a sequence of numbers such that the difference of any two successive members of the sequence is a constant.
    a. Arithmetic sequence0
    b. Thing
    c. Undefined
    d. Undefined

25. _____ is a branch of mathematics concerning the study of structure, relation and quantity.
    a. Algebra0
    b. Concept
    c. Undefined
    d. Undefined

26. In statistics, a _____ measure is one which is measuring what is supposed to measure.
    a. Valid0
    b. Thing
    c. Undefined
    d. Undefined

27. In mathematics and the mathematical sciences, a _____ is a fixed, but possibly unspecified, value. This is in contrast to a variable, which is not fixed.
    a. Constant0
    b. Thing
    c. Undefined
    d. Undefined

28. _____ the expected value of a random variable displays the average or central value of the variable. It is a summary value of the distribution of the variable.
    a. Determining0
    b. Thing
    c. Undefined
    d. Undefined

Chapter 8. Further Topics in Algebra

29. _____ is often used to describe the measurement of the steepness, incline, gradient, or grade of a straight line. The _____ is defined as the ratio of the "rise" divided by the "run" between two points on a line, or in other words, the ratio of the altitude change to the horizontal distance between any two points on the line.
   a. Slope0
   b. Thing
   c. Undefined
   d. Undefined

30. _____ means in succession or back-to-back
   a. Thing
   b. Consecutive0
   c. Undefined
   d. Undefined

31. A _____ is a sequence of numbers where each term after the first is found by multiplying the previous one by a fixed non-zero number called the common ratio.
   a. Thing
   b. Geometric sequence0
   c. Undefined
   d. Undefined

32. A _____ is a quantity that denotes the proportional amount or magnitude of one quantity relative to another.
   a. Thing
   b. Ratio0
   c. Undefined
   d. Undefined

33. In mathematics, _____ growth occurs when the growth rate of a function is always proportional to the function's current size.
   a. Exponential0
   b. Thing
   c. Undefined
   d. Undefined

34. _____ is one of the most important functions in mathematics. A function commonly used to study growth and decay
   a. Exponential function0
   b. Thing
   c. Undefined
   d. Undefined

35. _____ are the basic objects of study in graph theory. Informally speaking, a graph is a set of objects called points, nodes, or vertices connected by links called lines or edges.
   a. Thing
   b. Graphs0
   c. Undefined
   d. Undefined

36. A _____, scatter diagram or scatter graph is a graph used in statistics to visually display and relate two quantitative variables of a multidimensional data set by displaying the data as a collection of points, each having one coordinate on a horizontal and one on a vertical axis.
   a. Scatterplot0
   b. Thing
   c. Undefined
   d. Undefined

37. _____ is a synonym for information.
   a. Data0
   b. Thing
   c. Undefined
   d. Undefined

38. _____ is the process in which two clone daughter cells are produced by the cell division of one bacterium.

Chapter 8. Further Topics in Algebra

    a. Thing
    b. Bacteria growth0
    c. Undefined
    d. Undefined

39. _____ are a measure of time.
    a. Thing
    b. Minutes0
    c. Undefined
    d. Undefined

40. In elementary algebra, an _____ is a set that contains every real number between two indicated numbers and may contain the two numbers themselves.
    a. Thing
    b. Interval0
    c. Undefined
    d. Undefined

41. Initial objects are also called _____, and terminal objects are also called final.
    a. Thing
    b. Coterminal0
    c. Undefined
    d. Undefined

42. Pierre François _____ was a mathematician and a doctor in number theory from the University of Ghent in 1825.
    a. Verhulst0
    b. Person
    c. Undefined
    d. Undefined

43. In mathematics, a _____ is a mathematical statement which appears likely to be true, but has not been formally proven to be true under the rules of mathematical logic.
    a. Conjecture0
    b. Concept
    c. Undefined
    d. Undefined

44. Acid _____ ratio measures the ability of a company to use its near cash or quick assets to immediately extinguish its current liabilities.
    a. Thing
    b. Test0
    c. Undefined
    d. Undefined

45. Leonardo of Pisa (1170s or 1180s – 1250), also known as Leonardo Pisano, Leonardo Bonacci, Leonardo _____, or, most commonly, simply _____, was an Italian mathematician, considered by some "the most talented mathematician of the Middle Ages."
    a. Person
    b. Fibonacci0
    c. Undefined
    d. Undefined

46. In geometry, a _____ is defined as a quadrilateral where all four of its angles are right angles.
    a. Thing
    b. Rectangle0
    c. Undefined
    d. Undefined

47. In plane geometry, a _____ is a polygon with four equal sides, four right angles, and parallel opposite sides. In algebra, the _____ of a number is that number multiplied by itself.
    a. Square0
    b. Thing
    c. Undefined
    d. Undefined

48. In mathematics, a _____ of a number x is a number r such that r^2 = x, or in words, a number r whose square (the result of multiplying the number by itself) is x.
   a. Thing
   b. Square root0
   c. Undefined
   d. Undefined

49. In mathematics, a _____ of a complex-valued function f is a member x of the domain of f such that f(x) vanishes at x, that is, x : f (x) = 0.
   a. Thing
   b. Root0
   c. Undefined
   d. Undefined

50. A _____ is the result of the addition of a set of numbers. The numbers may be natural numbers, complex numbers, matrices, or still more complicated objects. An infinite _____ is a subtle procedure known as a series.
   a. Thing
   b. Sum0
   c. Undefined
   d. Undefined

51. A _____ is the sum of the elements of a sequence.
   a. Series0
   b. Thing
   c. Undefined
   d. Undefined

52. Mathematical _____ is used to represent ideas.
   a. Notation0
   b. Thing
   c. Undefined
   d. Undefined

53. _____ is the addition of a set of numbers; the result is their sum. The "numbers" to be summed may be natural numbers, complex numbers, matrices, or still more complicated objects. An infinite sum is a subtle procedure known as a series.
   a. Thing
   b. Summation0
   c. Undefined
   d. Undefined

54. _____ is an adjective usually refering to being in the centre.
   a. Central0
   b. Thing
   c. Undefined
   d. Undefined

55. In mathematics, a _____ is a countable collection of open covers of a topological space that satisfies certain separation axioms.
   a. Thing
   b. Development0
   c. Undefined
   d. Undefined

56. An _____ is a combination of numbers, operators, grouping symbols and/or free variables and bound variables arranged in a meaningful way which can be evaluated..
   a. Expression0
   b. Thing
   c. Undefined
   d. Undefined

57. _____ is often represented as the sum of a sequence of terms.

Chapter 8. Further Topics in Algebra

   a. Infinite series0
   b. Thing
   c. Undefined
   d. Undefined

58. In mathematics, an _____ number is any real number that is not a rational number- that is, it is a number which cannot be expressed as a fraction m/n, where m and n are integers.
   a. Thing
   b. Irrational0
   c. Undefined
   d. Undefined

59. In mathematics, an _____ is any real number that is not a rational number ¡ª that is, it is a number which cannot be expressed as m/n, where m and n are integers.
   a. Thing
   b. Irrational number0
   c. Undefined
   d. Undefined

60. An _____ of a product of sums expresses it as a sum of products by using the fact that multiplication distributes over addition.
   a. Thing
   b. Expansion0
   c. Undefined
   d. Undefined

61. _____ is the technique and science of accurately determining the terrestrial or three-dimensional space position of points and the distances and angles between them.
   a. Surveying0
   b. Thing
   c. Undefined
   d. Undefined

62. Compass and straightedge or ruler-and-compass _____ is the _____ of lengths or angles using only an idealized ruler and compass.
   a. Thing
   b. Construction0
   c. Undefined
   d. Undefined

63. The system of _____ numerals was a numeral system used in ancient Egypt. It was a decimal system, often rounded off to the higher power, written in hieroglyphs.
   a. Thing
   b. Egyptian0
   c. Undefined
   d. Undefined

64. _____ is a kind of property which exists as magnitude or multitude. It is among the basic classes of things along with quality, substance, change, and relation.
   a. Amount0
   b. Thing
   c. Undefined
   d. Undefined

65. In business, particularly accounting, a _____ is the time intervals that the accounts, statement, payments, or other calculations cover.
   a. Period0
   b. Thing
   c. Undefined
   d. Undefined

66. A _____ is a deliberate process for transforming one or more inputs into one or more results.

Chapter 8. Further Topics in Algebra

   a. Thing
   c. Undefined
   b. Calculation0
   d. Undefined

67. _____ is a term used in accounting, economics and finance with reference to the fact that assets with finite lives lose value over time.
   a. Depreciation0
   c. Undefined
   b. Thing
   d. Undefined

68. _____ is the income from capital investment paid in a series of regular payments.
   a. Annuity0
   c. Undefined
   b. Thing
   d. Undefined

69. _____ measures the nominal future sum of money that a given sum of money is "worth" at a specified time in the future assuming a certain interest rate; this value does not include corrections for inflation or other factors that affect the true value of money in the future.
   a. Future value0
   c. Undefined
   b. Thing
   d. Undefined

70. In mathematics, the _____ (or modulus) of a real number is its numerical value without regard to its sign.
   a. Thing
   c. Undefined
   b. Absolute value0
   d. Undefined

71. A _____ decimal is a number whose decimal representation eventually becomes periodic (i.e. the same number sequence _____ indefinitely).
   a. Repeating0
   c. Undefined
   b. Thing
   d. Undefined

72. Recurring or _____ are numbers which when expressed as decimals have a set of "final" digits which repeat an infinite number of times.
   a. Thing
   c. Undefined
   b. Repeating decimals0
   d. Undefined

73. _____ is the transport of people on a trip/journey or the process or time involved in a person or object moving from one location to another.
   a. Thing
   c. Undefined
   b. Travel0
   d. Undefined

74. A _____ is a unit of length, usually used to measure distance, in a number of different systems, including Imperial units, United States customary units and Norwegian/Swedish mil. Its size can vary from system to system, but in each is between 1 and 10 kilometers. In contemporary English contexts _____ refers to either:
   a. Thing
   c. Undefined
   b. Mile0
   d. Undefined

75. _____ is the eighteenth letter of the Greek alphabet.

140 Chapter 8. Further Topics in Algebra

  a. Thing
  b. Sigma0
  c. Undefined
  d. Undefined

76. The word _____ is used in a variety of ways in mathematics.
  a. Thing
  b. Index0
  c. Undefined
  d. Undefined

77. _____ is the distance around a given two-dimensional object. As a general rule, the _____ of a polygon can always be calculated by adding all the length of the sides together. So, the formula for triangles is P = a + b + c, where a, b and c stand for each side of it. For quadrilaterals the equation is P = a + b + c + d. For equilateral polygons, P = na, where n is the number of sides and a is the side length.
  a. Thing
  b. Perimeter0
  c. Undefined
  d. Undefined

78. In mathematics, a _____ number is a number which can be expressed as a ratio of two integers. Non-integer _____ numbers (commonly called fractions) are usually written as the vulgar fraction a / b, where b is not zero.
  a. Thing
  b. Rational0
  c. Undefined
  d. Undefined

79. _____, in economics and political economy, are the distributions or payments awarded to the various suppliers of the factors of production.
  a. Returns0
  b. Thing
  c. Undefined
  d. Undefined

80. A _____ signifies a point or points of probability on a subject e.g., the _____ of creativity, which allows for the formation of rule or norm or law by interpretation of the phenomena events that can be created.
  a. Principle0
  b. Thing
  c. Undefined
  d. Undefined

81. _____ is the mathematical action of repeatedly adding or subtracting one, usually to find out how many objects there are or to set aside a desired number of objects.
  a. Counting0
  b. Thing
  c. Undefined
  d. Undefined

82. In combinatorial mathematics, a _____ is an un-ordered collection of unique elements.
  a. Combination0
  b. Concept
  c. Undefined
  d. Undefined

83. _____ is the rearrangement of objects or symbols into distinguishable sequences.
  a. Permutation0
  b. Thing
  c. Undefined
  d. Undefined

84. The _____ is a method that is used to calculate all of the possibilities of a pertaining number of events.
  a. Fundamental Counting Principle0
  b. Thing
  c. Undefined
  d. Undefined

Chapter 8. Further Topics in Algebra

85. _____ is the chance that something is likely to happen or be the case.
    a. Thing
    b. Probability0
    c. Undefined
    d. Undefined

86. A _____ is a simplified and structured visual representation of concepts, ideas, constructions, relations, statistical data, anatomy etc used in all aspects of human activities to visualize and clarify the topic.
    a. Thing
    b. Diagram0
    c. Undefined
    d. Undefined

87. A _____ of a number is the product of that number with any integer.
    a. Multiple0
    b. Thing
    c. Undefined
    d. Undefined

88. In probability theory, _____ are various sets of outcomes (a subset of the sample space) to which a probability is assigned.
    a. Thing
    b. Events0
    c. Undefined
    d. Undefined

89. In mathematical logic, a Gödel numbering (or Gödel _____) is a function that assigns to each symbol and well-formed formula of some formal language a unique natural number called its Gödel number.
    a. Code0
    b. Thing
    c. Undefined
    d. Undefined

90. The _____ of a solid object is the three-dimensional concept of how much space it occupies, often quantified numerically.
    a. Thing
    b. Volume0
    c. Undefined
    d. Undefined

91. In physics, a _____ may refer to the scalar _____ or to the vector _____.
    a. Thing
    b. Potential0
    c. Undefined
    d. Undefined

92. Order theory is a branch of mathematics that studies various kinds of binary relations that capture the intuitive notion of a mathematical _____.
    a. Thing
    b. Ordering0
    c. Undefined
    d. Undefined

93. In mathematics, a _____ is the result of multiplying, or an expression that identifies factors to be multiplied.
    a. Thing
    b. Product0
    c. Undefined
    d. Undefined

94. _____ of a non-negative integer n is the product of all positive integers less than or equal to n.
    a. Factorial0
    b. Thing
    c. Undefined
    d. Undefined

Chapter 8. Further Topics in Algebra

95. A _____ is a negotiable instrument instructing a financial institution to pay a specific amount of a specific currency from a specific demand account held in the maker/depositor's name with that institution. Both the maker and payee may be natural persons or legal entities.
- a. Thing
- b. Check0
- c. Undefined
- d. Undefined

96. In Euclidean geometry, an _____ is a closed segment of a differentiable curve in the two-dimensional plane; for example, a circular _____ is a segment of a circle.
- a. Arc0
- b. Concept
- c. Undefined
- d. Undefined

97. In mathematics, factorization (British English: factorisation) or factoring is the decomposition of an object (for example, a number, a polynomial, or a matrix) into a product of other objects, or _____, which when multiplied together give the original.
- a. Thing
- b. Factors0
- c. Undefined
- d. Undefined

98. An _____ or member of a set is an object that when collected together make up the set.
- a. Element0
- b. Thing
- c. Undefined
- d. Undefined

99. In mathematics, the _____, or members of a set or more generally a class are all those objects which when collected together make up the set or class.
- a. Thing
- b. Elements0
- c. Undefined
- d. Undefined

100. A _____ is a set whose members are members of another set or a set contained within another set.
- a. Subset0
- b. Thing
- c. Undefined
- d. Undefined

101. _____ are groups whose members are members of another set or a set contained within another set.
- a. Thing
- b. Subsets0
- c. Undefined
- d. Undefined

102. In mathematics, a _____ is a condition that a solution to an optimization problem must satisfy in order to be acceptable.
- a. Constraint0
- b. Thing
- c. Undefined
- d. Undefined

103. The _____ is a popular form of gambling which involves the drawing of lots for a prize. Some governments forbid it, while others endorse it to the extent of organizign a national _____.
- a. Lottery0
- b. Thing
- c. Undefined
- d. Undefined

Chapter 8. Further Topics in Algebra

104. In mathematics and logic, a _____ proof is a way of showing the truth or falsehood of a given statement by a straightforward combination of established facts, usually existing lemmas and theorems, without making any further assumptions.
   a. Direct0
   b. Thing
   c. Undefined
   d. Undefined

105. The _____, the average in everyday English, which is also called the arithmetic _____ (and is distinguished from the geometric _____ or harmonic _____). The average is also called the sample _____. The expected value of a random variable, which is also called the population _____.
   a. Mean0
   b. Thing
   c. Undefined
   d. Undefined

106. In Euclidean geometry, a _____ is the set of all points in a plane at a fixed distance, called the radius, from a given point, the center.
   a. Circle0
   b. Thing
   c. Undefined
   d. Undefined

107. Multiple Signal Classification, also known as _____, is an algorithm used for frequency estimation and emitter location.
   a. Thing
   b. Music0
   c. Undefined
   d. Undefined

108. _____ is a mathematical subject that includes the study of limits, derivatives, integrals, and power series and constitutes a major part of modern university curriculum.
   a. Calculus0
   b. Thing
   c. Undefined
   d. Undefined

109. In mathematics, a _____ or rhodonea curve is a sinusoid plotted in polar coordinates.
   a. Thing
   b. Rose0
   c. Undefined
   d. Undefined

110. In mathematics, the _____ is an important formula giving the expansion of powers of sums.
   a. Binomial Theorem0
   b. Thing
   c. Undefined
   d. Undefined

111. In mathematics, a _____ is a statement that can be proved on the basis of explicitly stated or previously agreed assumptions.
   a. Theorem0
   b. Thing
   c. Undefined
   d. Undefined

112. In elementary algebra, a _____ is a polynomial with two terms: the sum of two monomials. It is the simplest kind of polynomial except for a monomial.
   a. Thing
   b. Binomial0
   c. Undefined
   d. Undefined

Chapter 8. Further Topics in Algebra

113. A _____ is a symbolic representation denoting a quantity or expression. It often represents an "unknown" quantity that has the potential to change.
   a. Variable0
   b. Thing
   c. Undefined
   d. Undefined

114. A _____ is one of the basic shapes of geometry: a polygon with three vertices and three sides which are straight line segments.
   a. Triangle0
   b. Thing
   c. Undefined
   d. Undefined

115. Blaise _____ was a French mathematician, physicist, and religious philosopher.
   a. Person
   b. Pascal0
   c. Undefined
   d. Undefined

116. In mathematics, a _____ is a constant multiplicative factor of a certain object. The object can be such things as a variable, a vector, a function, etc. For example, the _____ of $9x^2$ is 9.
   a. Coefficient0
   b. Thing
   c. Undefined
   d. Undefined

117. In mathematics, particularly in combinatorics, the _____ of the natural number n and the integer k is the number of combinations that exist.
   a. Thing
   b. Binomial coefficient0
   c. Undefined
   d. Undefined

118. _____ has many meanings, most of which simply .
   a. Thing
   b. Power0
   c. Undefined
   d. Undefined

119. In mathematics, a _____ is a demonstration that, assuming certain axioms, some statement is necessarily true.
   a. Thing
   b. Proof0
   c. Undefined
   d. Undefined

120. _____ is a method of mathematical proof typically used to establish that a given statement is true of all natural numbers
   a. Mathematical induction0
   b. Thing
   c. Undefined
   d. Undefined

121. Johann _____ was a German mathematician and scientist of profound genius who contributed significantly to many fields, including number theory, analysis, differential geometry, geodesy, magnetism, astronomy, and optics. He completed Disquisitiones Arithmeticae, his magnum opus, at the age of twenty-one.
   a. Person
   b. Carl Friedrich Gauss0
   c. Undefined
   d. Undefined

Chapter 8. Further Topics in Algebra

122. The _____ are the only integral domain whose positive elements are well-ordered, and in which order is preserved by addition. Like the natural numbers, the _____ form a countably infinite set. The set of all _____ is usually denoted in mathematics by a boldface Z .
   a. Thing
   b. Integers0
   c. Undefined
   d. Undefined

123. In common philosophical language, a proposition or _____, is the content of an assertion, that is, it is true-or-false and defined by the meaning of a particular piece of language.
   a. Concept
   b. Statement0
   c. Undefined
   d. Undefined

124. Two mathematical objects are equal if and only if they are precisely the same in every way. This defines a binary relation, _____, denoted by the sign of _____ "=" in such a way that the statement "x = y" means that x and y are equal.
   a. Thing
   b. Equality0
   c. Undefined
   d. Undefined

125. In mathematics, a _____ may be described informally as a number that can be given by an infinite decimal representation.
   a. Thing
   b. Real number0
   c. Undefined
   d. Undefined

126. In mathematics, an _____ is a statement about the relative size or order of two objects.
   a. Thing
   b. Inequality0
   c. Undefined
   d. Undefined

127. In mathematics, an inequality is a statement about the relative size or order of two objects. For example 14 > 10, or 14 is _____ 10.
   a. Greater than0
   b. Thing
   c. Undefined
   d. Undefined

128. The deductive-nomological model is a formalized view of scientific _____ in natural language.
   a. Explanation0
   b. Thing
   c. Undefined
   d. Undefined

129. In mathematics, a _____ is an algebraic structure in which addition and multiplication are defined and have properties listed below.
   a. Thing
   b. Ring0
   c. Undefined
   d. Undefined

130. _____ interest refers to the fact that whenever interest is calculated, it is based not only on the original principal, but also on any unpaid interest that has been added to the principal.
   a. Thing
   b. Compound0
   c. Undefined
   d. Undefined

131. _____ was a French mathematician, physicist, and religious philosopher.

a. Blaise Pascal0
c. Undefined
b. Person
d. Undefined

132. A _____ is a function that assigns a number to subsets of a given set.
 a. Thing
 b. Measure0
 c. Undefined
 d. Undefined

133. In the scientific method, an _____ (Latin: ex-+-periri, "of (or from) trying"), is a set of actions and observations, performed in the context of solving a particular problem or question, in order to support or falsify a hypothesis or research concerning phenomena.
 a. Experiment0
 b. Thing
 c. Undefined
 d. Undefined

134. _____ is a set, with some particular properties and usually some additional structure, such as the operations of addition or multiplication, for instance.
 a. Space0
 b. Thing
 c. Undefined
 d. Undefined

135. _____ is a subset of a population.
 a. Sample0
 b. Thing
 c. Undefined
 d. Undefined

136. In probability theory, the _____ or universal _____, often denoted S, Ù or U (for "universe"), of an experiment or random trial is the set of all possible outcomes.
 a. Thing
 b. Sample space0
 c. Undefined
 d. Undefined

137. If the probabilities of simple events are all the same, then they are _____. This occurs in a uniform sample space.
 a. Equally likely0
 b. Thing
 c. Undefined
 d. Undefined

138. In set theory and other branches of mathematics, the _____ of a collection of sets is the set that contains everything that belongs to any of the sets, but nothing else.
 a. Union0
 b. Thing
 c. Undefined
 d. Undefined

139. In set theory and other branches of mathematics, two kinds of complements are defined, the relative _____ and the absolute _____.
 a. Thing
 b. Complement0
 c. Undefined
 d. Undefined

140. In mathematics, two sets are said to be _____ if they have no element in common. For example, {1, 2, 3} and {4, 5, 6} are sets which are _____.

Chapter 8. Further Topics in Algebra

    a. Disjoint0
    c. Undefined
    b. Thing
    d. Undefined

141. _____ is a branch of mathematics which deals with triangles, particularly triangles in a plane where one angle of the triangle is 90 degrees, and a variety of other topological relations such as spheres, in other branches, such as spherical _____.
    a. Thing
    c. Undefined
    b. Trigonometry0
    d. Undefined

142. In mathematics, the _____ of two sets A and B is the set that contains all elements of A that also belong to B (or equivalently, all elements of B that also belong to A), but no other elements.
    a. Intersection0
    c. Undefined
    b. Thing
    d. Undefined

143. In logic, two _____ (or "mutual exclusive" according to some sources) propositions are propositions that logically cannot both be true.
    a. Concept
    c. Undefined
    b. Mutually exclusive0
    d. Undefined

144. The material _____, also known as the material implication or truth functional _____, expresses a property of certain conditionals in logic.
    a. Thing
    c. Undefined
    b. Conditional0
    d. Undefined

145. _____ is the probability of some event A, given the occurrence of some other event B.
    a. Thing
    c. Undefined
    b. Conditional probability0
    d. Undefined

146. There are two main approaches to _____ in mathematics. They are the model theory of _____ and the proof theory of _____.
    a. Truth0
    c. Undefined
    b. Thing
    d. Undefined

147. _____ is electromagnetic radiation with a wavelength that is visible to the eye (visible _____) or, in a technical or scientific context, electromagnetic radiation of any wavelength.
    a. Light0
    c. Undefined
    b. Thing
    d. Undefined

148. A _____ is an illustration used in the branch of mathematics known as set theory. It shows all of the possible mathematical or logical relationships between sets.
    a. Thing
    c. Undefined
    b. Venn diagram0
    d. Undefined

149. In set theory and its applications throughout mathematics, _____ are a collection of sets (or sometimes other mathematical objects) that can be unambiguously defined by a property that all its members share.

a. Classes0 b. Thing
c. Undefined d. Undefined

150. In mathematics, the concept of a _____ tries to capture the intuitive idea of a geometrical one-dimensional and continuous object. A simple example is the circle.
   a. Curve0 b. Thing
   c. Undefined d. Undefined

151. In mathematics, a _____ is a rectangular table of numbers or, more generally, a table consisting of abstract quantities that can be added and multiplied.
   a. Matrix0 b. Thing
   c. Undefined d. Undefined

152. _____ is the design, analysis, and/or construction of works for practical purposes.
   a. Thing b. Engineering0
   c. Undefined d. Undefined

153. _____ is a notation for writing numbers that is often used by scientists and mathematicians to make it easier to write large and small numbers.
   a. Scientific notation0 b. Thing
   c. Undefined d. Undefined

154. In mathematics, the _____ of a function is the set of all "output" values produced by that function. Given a function $f: A \to B$, the _____ of f, is defined to be the set $\{x \in B : x = f(a)$ for some $a \in A\}$.
   a. Range0 b. Thing
   c. Undefined d. Undefined

155. _____ is the notation in which permitted values for a variable are expressed as ranging over a certain interval; "5 < x < 9" is an example of the application of _____.
   a. Thing b. Interval notation0
   c. Undefined d. Undefined

156. In geometry, two lines or planes if one falls on the other in such a way as to create congruent adjacent angles. The term may be used as a noun or adjective. Thus, referring to Figure 1, the line AB is the _____ to CD through the point B.
   a. Thing b. Perpendicular0
   c. Undefined d. Undefined

157. _____ systems represent systems whose behavior is not expressible as a sum of the behaviors of its descriptors.
   a. Thing b. Nonlinear0
   c. Undefined d. Undefined

158. In geometry, a _____ is a special kind of point, usually a corner of a polygon, polyhedron, or higher dimensional polytope. In the geometry of curves a _____ is a point of where the first derivative of curvature is zero. In graph theory, a _____ is the fundamental unit out of which graphs are formed

Chapter 8. Further Topics in Algebra

    a. Vertex0
    c. Undefined
    b. Thing
    d. Undefined

159. _____ of a polynomial with real or complex coefficients is a certain expression in the coefficients of the polynomial which is equal to zero if and only if the polynomial has a multiple root i.e. a root with multiplicity greater than one in the complex numbers.
    a. Discriminant0
    c. Undefined
    b. Thing
    d. Undefined

160. The _____ of a member of a multiset is how many memberships in the multiset it has.
    a. Thing
    c. Undefined
    b. Multiplicity0
    d. Undefined

161. A _____ is a set of numbers that designate location in a given reference system, such as x,y in a planar _____ system or an x,y,z in a three-dimensional _____ system.
    a. Thing
    c. Undefined
    b. Coordinate0
    d. Undefined

162. in mathematics, maxima and minima, known collectively as _____, are the largest value maximum or smallest value minimum, that a function takes in a point either within a given neighborhood or on the function domain in its entirety global extremum.
    a. Extrema0
    c. Undefined
    b. Thing
    d. Undefined

163. A real-valued function f defined on the real line is said to have a _____ point at the point x∗, if there exists some ε > 0, such that f when x − x∗ < ε.
    a. Thing
    c. Undefined
    b. Local maximum0
    d. Undefined

164. In mathematics, there are several meanings of _____ depending on the subject.
    a. Degree0
    c. Undefined
    b. Thing
    d. Undefined

165. In mathematics, a _____ is a polynomial equation of the second degree. The general form is $ax^2 + bx + c = 0$.
    a. Quadratic equation0
    c. Undefined
    b. Thing
    d. Undefined

166. An _____ is a straight line or curve A to which another curve B approaches closer and closer as one moves along it. As one moves along B, the space between it and the _____ A becomes smaller and smaller, and can in fact be made as small as one could wish by going far enough along. A curve may or may not touch or cross its _____. In fact, the curve may intersect the _____ an infinite number of times.
    a. Asymptote0
    c. Undefined
    b. Thing
    d. Undefined

167. In astronomy, geography, geometry and related sciences and contexts, a plane is said to be _____ at a given point if it is locally perpendicular to the gradient of the gravity field, i.e., with the direction of the gravitational force at that point.

Chapter 8. Further Topics in Algebra

    a. Thing
    b. Horizontal0
    c. Undefined
    d. Undefined

168. In mathematics, an _____ number is a complex number whose square is a negative real number. They were defined in 1572 by Rafael Bombelli.
    a. Imaginary0
    b. Thing
    c. Undefined
    d. Undefined

169. _____ is a function of the form
    a. Cubic function0
    b. Thing
    c. Undefined
    d. Undefined

170. An _____ is when two lines intersect somewhere on a plane creating a right angle at intersection
    a. Axes0
    b. Thing
    c. Undefined
    d. Undefined

171. In mathematics, a _____ of a number x is the exponent y of the power by such that $x = b^y$. The value used for the base b must be neither 0 nor 1, nor a root of 1 in the case of the extension to complex numbers, and is typically 10, e, or 2.
    a. Thing
    b. Logarithm0
    c. Undefined
    d. Undefined

172. A _____ is a set of possible values that a variable can take on in order to satisfy a given set of conditions, which may include equations and inequalities.
    a. Thing
    b. Solution set0
    c. Undefined
    d. Undefined

173. In mathematics, an _____ .
    a. Ellipse0
    b. Thing
    c. Undefined
    d. Undefined

174. In mathematics, the _____ is a conic section generated by the intersection of a right circular conical surface and a plane parallel to a generating straight line of that surface. It can also be defined as locus of points in a plane which are equidistant from a given point.
    a. Parabola0
    b. Thing
    c. Undefined
    d. Undefined

175. In mathematics, a _____ is a type of conic section defined as the intersection between a right circular conical surface and a plane which cuts through both halves of the cone.
    a. Thing
    b. Hyperbola0
    c. Undefined
    d. Undefined

176. In geometry, the _____ are a pair of special points used in describing conic sections. The four types of conic sections are the circle, parabola, ellipse, and hyperbola.
    a. Foci0
    b. Thing
    c. Undefined
    d. Undefined

Chapter 8. Further Topics in Algebra

177. In classical geometry, a _____ of a circle or sphere is any line segment from its center to its boundary. By extension, the _____ of a circle or sphere is the length of any such segment. The _____ is half the diameter. In science and engineering the term _____ of curvature is commonly used as a synonym for _____.
   a. Radius0
   b. Thing
   c. Undefined
   d. Undefined

178. A _____ is a three-dimensional geometric shape formed by straight lines through a fixed point (vertex) to the points of a fixed curve (directrix)
   a. Cone0
   b. Concept
   c. Undefined
   d. Undefined

179. _____ is a unit of speed, expressing the number of international miles covered per hour.
   a. Miles per hour0
   b. Thing
   c. Undefined
   d. Undefined

180. A _____ is a special kind of ratio, indicating a relationship between two measurements with different units, such as miles to gallons or cents to pounds.
   a. Rate0
   b. Thing
   c. Undefined
   d. Undefined

181. A _____ is a polynomial function of the form f(x) = ax^2 + bx +c , where a, b, c are real numbers and a , 0.
   a. Event
   b. Quadratic function0
   c. Undefined
   d. Undefined

182. In geometry, a _____ (Greek words diairo = divide and metro = measure) of a circle is any straight line segment that passes through the centre and whose endpoints are on the circular boundary, or, in more modern usage, the length of such a line segment. When using the word in the more modern sense, one speaks of the _____ rather than a _____, because all diameters of a circle have the same length. This length is twice the radius. The _____ of a circle is also the longest chord that the circle has.
   a. Diameter0
   b. Thing
   c. Undefined
   d. Undefined

183. _____ are external two-dimensional outlines, with the appearance or configuration of some thing - in contrast to the matter or content or substance of which it is composed.
   a. Shapes0
   b. Thing
   c. Undefined
   d. Undefined

184. In mathematics, a _____ is a two-dimensional manifold or surface that is perfectly flat.
   a. Plane0
   b. Thing
   c. Undefined
   d. Undefined

185. _____ is a relation in Euclidean geometry among the three sides of a right triangle.
   a. Pythagorean Theorem0
   b. Thing
   c. Undefined
   d. Undefined

186. A frame of _____ is a particular perspective from which the universe is observed.

Chapter 8. Further Topics in Algebra

a. Reference0
b. Thing
c. Undefined
d. Undefined

187. _____ has one 90° internal angle a right angle.
  a. Thing
  b. Right triangle0
  c. Undefined
  d. Undefined

188. In a right triangle, the _____ of the triangle are the two sides that are perpendicular to each other, as opposed to the hypotenuse.
  a. Thing
  b. Legs0
  c. Undefined
  d. Undefined

189. The _____ is the distance around a closed curve. _____ is a kind of perimeter.
  a. Circumference0
  b. Thing
  c. Undefined
  d. Undefined

190. The metre (or _____, see spelling differences) is a measure of length. It is the basic unit of length in the metric system and in the International System of Units (SI), used around the world for general and scientific purposes.
  a. Meter0
  b. Concept
  c. Undefined
  d. Undefined

191. The _____ of measurement are a globally standardized and modernized form of the metric system.
  a. Units0
  b. Thing
  c. Undefined
  d. Undefined

192. In mathematics, a _____ is the set of all points in three-dimensional space (R^3) which are at distance r from a fixed point of that space, where r is a positive real number called the radius of the _____. The fixed point is called the center or centre, and is not part of the _____ itself.
  a. Sphere0
  b. Thing
  c. Undefined
  d. Undefined

193. _____ are cubes in which all sides are of the same length and all face perpendicular to each other including an atom at each corner of the unigt cell.
  a. Thing
  b. Cubic units0
  c. Undefined
  d. Undefined

194. In mathematics, a _____ is a quadric surface, with the following equation in Cartesian coordinates: $(x/_a)^2 + (y/_b)^2 = 1$.
  a. Thing
  b. Cylinder0
  c. Undefined
  d. Undefined

195. A _____ surface is the surface or face of a solid on its sides. It can also be defined as any face or surface that is not a base.
  a. Lateral0
  b. Thing
  c. Undefined
  d. Undefined

Chapter 8. Further Topics in Algebra

196. In geometry, two sets are called _____ if one can be transformed into the other by an isometry, i.e., a combination of translations, rotations and reflections.
  a. Thing
  b. Congruent0
  c. Undefined
  d. Undefined

197. In mathematics, a _____ is an n-tuple with n being 3.
  a. Thing
  b. Triple0
  c. Undefined
  d. Undefined

198. The plus and _____ signs are mathematical symbols used to represent the notions of positive and negative as well as the operations of addition and subtraction.
  a. Minus0
  b. Thing
  c. Undefined
  d. Undefined

199. A _____ is a unit of length in the metric system, equal to one thousand metres, the current SI base unit of length
  a. Kilometer0
  b. Thing
  c. Undefined
  d. Undefined

200. The _____ of a right triangle is the triangle's longest side; the side opposite the right angle.
  a. Hypotenuse0
  b. Thing
  c. Undefined
  d. Undefined

201. The _____ (symbol _____) and the millibar (symbol mbar, also mb) are units of pressure.
  a. Thing
  b. Bar0
  c. Undefined
  d. Undefined

202. In geometry, the _____ of an object is a point in some sense in the middle of the object.
  a. Center0
  b. Thing
  c. Undefined
  d. Undefined

203. In geometry, an _____ is a point at which a line segment or ray terminates.
  a. Endpoint0
  b. Thing
  c. Undefined
  d. Undefined

204. In mathematics, a _____ is the end result of a division problem. It can also be expressed as the number of times the divisor divides into the dividend.
  a. Thing
  b. Quotient0
  c. Undefined
  d. Undefined

205. _____ is a mathematical operation, written a^n, involving two numbers, the base a and the exponent n.
  a. Exponentiating0
  b. Thing
  c. Undefined
  d. Undefined

206. _____ is a mathematical operation, written a^n, involving two numbers, the base a and the exponent n.

Chapter 8. Further Topics in Algebra

a. Exponentiation0
b. Thing
c. Undefined
d. Undefined

207. A _____ is a three-dimensional solid object bounded by six square faces, facets, or sides, with three meeting at each vertex.
a. Thing
b. Cube0
c. Undefined
d. Undefined

208. The _____ governs the differentiation of products of differentiable functions.
a. Thing
b. Product rule0
c. Undefined
d. Undefined

209. In mathematics, _____ expressions is used to reduce the expression into the lowest possible term.
a. Simplifying0
b. Thing
c. Undefined
d. Undefined

210. A _____ is a numeral used to indicate a count. The most common use of the word today is to name the part of a fraction that tells the number or count of equal parts.
a. Numerator0
b. Thing
c. Undefined
d. Undefined

211. The _____ is a method of finding the derivative of a function that is the quotient of two other functions for which derivatives exist.
a. Thing
b. Quotient rule0
c. Undefined
d. Undefined

212. _____ is a method for differentiating expressions involving exponentiation the power operation.
a. Power rule0
b. Thing
c. Undefined
d. Undefined

213. In mathematics, a _____ is a particular kind of polynomial, having just one term.
a. Monomial0
b. Thing
c. Undefined
d. Undefined

214. In mathematics, a _____ is an expression that is constructed from one or more variables and constants, using only the operations of addition, subtraction, multiplication, and constant positive whole number exponents. is a _____. Note in particular that division by an expression containing a variable is not in general allowed in polynomials. [1]
a. Polynomial0
b. Thing
c. Undefined
d. Undefined

215. In mathematics, _____ is an elementary arithmetic operation. When one of the numbers is a whole number, _____ is the repeated sum of the other number.
a. Multiplication0
b. Thing
c. Undefined
d. Undefined

216. The _____ integers are all the integers from zero on upwards.

Chapter 8. Further Topics in Algebra

a. Nonnegative0
b. Thing
c. Undefined
d. Undefined

217. The _____ is the maximum of the degrees of all terms in the polynomial.
   a. Degree of a polynomial0
   b. Thing
   c. Undefined
   d. Undefined

218. In mathematics, the additive inverse, or _____ of a number n is the number that, when added to n, yields zero. The additive inverse of n is denoted −n. For example, 7 is −7, because 7 + (−7) = 0, and the additive inverse of −0.3 is 0.3, because −0.3 + 0.3 = 0.
   a. Thing
   b. Opposite0
   c. Undefined
   d. Undefined

219. _____ element of an element x with respect to a binary operation * with identity element e is an element y such that x * y = y * x = e. In particular,
   a. Inverse0
   b. Thing
   c. Undefined
   d. Undefined

220. In mathematics, the _____ inverse, or opposite, of a number n is the number that, when added to n, yields zero. The _____ inverse of n is denoted −n.
   a. Additive0
   b. Thing
   c. Undefined
   d. Undefined

221. In mathematics, the _____ of a number n is the number that, when added to n, yields zero. The _____ of n is denoted −n. For example, 7 is −7, because 7 + (−7) = 0, and the _____ of −0.3 is 0.3, because −0.3 + 0.3 = 0.
   a. Thing
   b. Additive inverse0
   c. Undefined
   d. Undefined

222. In mathematics, and in particular in abstract algebra, the _____ is a property of binary operations that generalises the distributive law from elementary algebra.
   a. Thing
   b. Distributive property0
   c. Undefined
   d. Undefined

223. In mathematics, _____ is the decomposition of an object into a product of other objects, or factors, which when multiplied together give the original.
   a. Factoring0
   b. Thing
   c. Undefined
   d. Undefined

224. A _____ is a polynomial consisting of three terms; in other words, it is the sum of three monomials.
   a. Trinomial0
   b. Thing
   c. Undefined
   d. Undefined

225. _____ are of a number n in its third power-the result of multiplying it by itself three times.
   a. Cubes0
   b. Thing
   c. Undefined
   d. Undefined

Chapter 8. Further Topics in Algebra

226. In abstract algebra, _____ consists of sets with binary operations that satisfy certain axioms.
   a. Grouping0
   b. Thing
   c. Undefined
   d. Undefined

227. _____ is the largest positive integer that divides both numbers without remainder.
   a. Thing
   b. Common Factor0
   c. Undefined
   d. Undefined

228. The term _____ can refer to an integer which is the square of some other integer, or an algebraic expression that can be factored as the square of some other expression.
   a. Thing
   b. Perfect square0
   c. Undefined
   d. Undefined

229. In mathematics the _____ refers to the identity: $a^2 - b^2 = (a+b)(a-b)$
   a. Difference of two squares0
   b. Thing
   c. Undefined
   d. Undefined

230. _____, either of the curved-bracket punctuation marks that together make a set of _____
   a. Parentheses0
   b. Thing
   c. Undefined
   d. Undefined

231. In mathematics, _____ is a property that a binary operation can have. Within an expression containing two or more of the same associative operators in a row, the order of operations does not matter as long as the sequence of the operands is not changed.
   a. Associativity0
   b. Thing
   c. Undefined
   d. Undefined

232. A _____ fraction is a fraction in which the absolute value of the numerator is less than the denominator--hence, the absolute value of the fraction is less than 1.
   a. Thing
   b. Proper0
   c. Undefined
   d. Undefined

233. _____ also sometimes known as the double distributive property or more colloquially as foiling, is commonly taught to US high school students learning algebra as a mnemonic for remembering how to multiply two binomials polynomials with two terms.
   a. Thing
   b. FOIL method0
   c. Undefined
   d. Undefined

234. The _____ is commonly taught to US high school students learning algebra as a mnemonic for remembering how to multiply two binomials.
   a. Thing
   b. FOIL rule0
   c. Undefined
   d. Undefined

235. _____ is a general method of problem solving for obtaining knowledge, both propositional and know-how. It is used typically in elementary algebra, when solving equations.

Chapter 8. Further Topics in Algebra

    a. Thing
    c. Undefined
    b. Guess and check0
    d. Undefined

236. In mathematics, the _____ divisor of two non-zero integers, is the largest positive integer that divides both numbers without remainder.
    a. Thing
    c. Undefined
    b. Greatest common0
    d. Undefined

237. In Math the greates common divisor sometimes known as the _____ of two non- zero integers.
    a. Greatest common factor0
    c. Undefined
    b. Thing
    d. Undefined

238. A _____ is the part of a fraction that tells how many equal parts make up a whole, and which is used in the name of the fraction: "halves", "thirds", "fourths" or "quarters", "fifths" and so on.
    a. Denominator0
    c. Undefined
    b. Concept
    d. Undefined

239. In mathematics, the multiplicative inverse of a number x, denoted $1/x$ or x^{-1}, is the number which, when multiplied by x, yields 1. The multiplicative inverse of x is also called the _____ of x.
    a. Thing
    c. Undefined
    b. Reciprocal0
    d. Undefined

240. In mathematics, a _____ of an integer n, also called a factor of n, is an integer which evenly divides n without leaving a remainder.
    a. Divisor0
    c. Undefined
    b. Thing
    d. Undefined

241. The _____ of two integers is the smallest positive integer that is a multiple of both intergers.
    a. Least common multiple0
    c. Undefined
    b. Thing
    d. Undefined

242. _____ is the symbold used to indicate the nth root of a number
    a. Thing
    c. Undefined
    b. Radical0
    d. Undefined

243. The _____ is the number or expression underneath the radical sign.
    a. Radicand0
    c. Undefined
    b. Thing
    d. Undefined

244. A _____ of a number is a number a such that $a^3 = x$.
    a. Thing
    c. Undefined
    b. Cube root0
    d. Undefined

245. A _____ is a number that is less than zero.

Chapter 8. Further Topics in Algebra

a. Negative number
b. Thing
c. Undefined
d. Undefined

246. An _____ of a number a is a number b such that $b^n = a$.
a. Thing
b. Nth root
c. Undefined
d. Undefined

247. In mathematics, _____ are used to indicate the square root of a number.
a. Thing
b. Radicals
c. Undefined
d. Undefined

248. A _____ is a number which is the cube of an integer.
a. Thing
b. Perfect cube
c. Undefined
d. Undefined

249. _____, or Rationalisation in mathematics is the process of removing a square root or imaginary number from the denominator of a fraction.
a. Thing
b. Rationalizing
c. Undefined
d. Undefined

250. In algebra, a _____ is a binomial formed by taking the opposite of the second term of a binomial.
a. Conjugate
b. Thing
c. Undefined
d. Undefined

ANSWER KEY

Chapter 1

1. b	2. b	3. a	4. b	5. b	6. b	7. a	8. a	9. b	10. b
11. a	12. b	13. a	14. b	15. a	16. a	17. b	18. a	19. b	20. a
21. b	22. a	23. a	24. a	25. a	26. b	27. a	28. a	29. b	30. b
31. b	32. a	33. b	34. b	35. a	36. b	37. b	38. a	39. b	40. a
41. a	42. b	43. a	44. b	45. a	46. a	47. b	48. b	49. a	50. a
51. a	52. b	53. a	54. a	55. a	56. a	57. a	58. b	59. b	60. a
61. b	62. a	63. b	64. b	65. b	66. b	67. b	68. b	69. b	70. b
71. a	72. a	73. a	74. a	75. b	76. b	77. a	78. a	79. a	80. a
81. b	82. b	83. a	84. a	85. b	86. a	87. b	88. b	89. b	90. b
91. a	92. a	93. b	94. b	95. a	96. a	97. b	98. b	99. b	100. a
101. b	102. a	103. b	104. b	105. a	106. b	107. a	108. b	109. b	110. b
111. b	112. a	113. a	114. b	115. a	116. a	117. a	118. b	119. a	120. b
121. a	122. a	123. a	124. b	125. b	126. b	127. a	128. b	129. b	130. b
131. a	132. b	133. b	134. b	135. a	136. b	137. a	138. a	139. a	140.
141. b	142. a	143. a	144.	145. a	146. a	147. a	148.	149. a	150. b
151. b	152. b	153. b	154. b	155. a	156. b	157. b	158. b	159. b	160. a
161. a	162. b	163. a	164. a	165. a	166. a	167. b	168. b	169. a	170. b
171. b	172. a	173. b	174. a	175. a	176. b	177. b	178. b	179. a	180. b

Chapter 2

1. b	2. b	3. b	4. b	5. a	6. b	7. b	8. a	9. b	10. a
11. a	12. a	13. b	14. b	15. b	16. b	17. a	18. b	19. b	20. a
21. a	22. a	23. b	24. b	25. b	26. b	27. a	28. a	29. b	30. b
31. b	32. a	33. b	34. a	35. a	36. b	37. b	38. b	39. a	40. a
41. b	42. a	43. a	44. a	45. a	46. a	47. a	48. a	49. b	50. b
51. a	52. a	53. a	54. a	55. a	56. a	57. a	58. b	59. a	60. a
61. a	62. a	63. a	64. b	65. b	66. a	67. b	68. a	69. b	70. a
71. a	72. b	73. b	74. a	75. b	76. a	77. b	78. a	79. a	80. a
81. b	82. b	83. a	84. a	85. b	86. a	87. b	88. b	89. b	90. a
91. b	92. b	93. b	94. a	95. b	96. b	97. a	98. a	99. b	100. b
101. a	102. a	103. b	104. b	105. a	106. a	107. b	108. b	109. b	110. b
111. a	112. a	113. a	114. b	115. a	116. b	117. b	118. a	119. b	120. b
121. b	122. a	123. a	124. a	125. b	126. a	127. b	128. b	129. a	130. b
131. a	132. b	133. b	134. a	135. a	136. b	137. b	138. b	139. a	140. b
141. b	142. a	143. b	144. a	145. a	146. b	147. a	148. b	149. b	150. b
151. a	152. a	153. b	154. a	155. b	156. b	157. b	158. b	159. a	160. a
161. a	162. a	163. a	164. b	165. b	166. b	167. a	168. a	169. b	170. a
171. b	172. a	173. b	174. b	175. b	176. b	177. b	178. b	179. b	180. a

Chapter 3

1. a	2. b	3. b	4. a	5. a	6. b	7. a	8. a	9. b	10. a
11. b	12. b	13. a	14. b	15. a	16. a	17. b	18. a	19. b	20. b
21. b	22. a	23. a	24. a	25. b	26. a	27. a	28. a	29. b	30. a
31. a	32. b	33. a	34. b	35. b	36. b	37. b	38. b	39. a	40. a
41. b	42. b	43. b	44. a	45. a	46. b	47. b	48. b	49. a	50. a
51. a	52. b	53. b	54. a	55. a	56. b	57. a	58. a	59. a	60. b
61. b	62. b	63. b	64. b	65. b	66. a	67. a	68. b	69. a	70. a
71. b	72. b	73. b	74. a	75. a	76. b	77. a	78. b	79. b	80. a
81. b	82. a	83. b	84. a	85. a	86. a	87. b	88. a	89. b	90. a
91. a	92. a	93. a	94. a	95. a	96. b	97. b	98. b	99. b	100. b
101. b	102. b	103. a	104. a	105. a	106. a	107. a	108. a	109. b	110. a
111. b	112. a	113. b	114. a	115. a	116. a	117. a	118. b	119. b	120. b
121. b	122. b	123. b	124. b	125. b	126. a	127. a	128. b	129. b	130. b
131. b	132. a	133. a	134. a	135. b	136. a	137. a			

Chapter 4

1. b	2. b	3. b	4. b	5. b	6. a	7. b	8. a	9. a	10. a
11. b	12. a	13. b	14. a	15. a	16. a	17. a	18. a	19. b	20. b
21. b	22. a	23. a	24. b	25. a	26. b	27. b	28. a	29. b	30. a
31. b	32. a	33. a	34. b	35. b	36. a	37. a	38. a	39. a	40. a
41. b	42. a	43. a	44. b	45. b	46. a	47. b	48. a	49. a	50. a
51. b	52. a	53. a	54. b	55. a	56. b	57. b	58. b	59. b	60. a
61. b	62. a	63. b	64. b	65. a	66. a	67. a	68. a	69. a	70. b
71. b	72. b	73. a	74. b	75. b	76. a	77. b	78. a	79. a	80. b
81. b	82. a	83. a	84. a	85. b	86. a	87. a	88. a	89. b	90. a
91. b	92. a	93. b	94. a	95. a	96. a	97. b	98. b	99. b	100. b
101. b	102. b	103. a	104. a	105. b	106. a	107. b	108. b	109. a	110. b
111. a	112. a	113. b	114. a	115. b	116. b	117. b	118. a	119. b	120. a
121. b	122. a	123. b	124. b	125. b	126. b	127. a	128. a	129. b	130. b
131. b	132. a	133. b	134. a	135. b	136. b	137. a	138. a	139. a	140. b
141. b	142. b	143. b	144. b	145. b	146. a	147. a	148. b	149. b	150. b
151. b	152. b	153. a	154. a	155. a	156. a	157. a	158. a	159. b	160. b
161. b	162. b	163. b	164. b	165. b	166. b	167. a	168. a	169. a	170. a
171. a	172. b	173. b	174. a	175. a	176. a	177. a	178. b	179. a	180. a
181. a	182. b	183. a	184. b	185. b	186. a	187. b	188. b	189. a	190. a
191. b	192. a	193. a	194. a	195. b	196. b	197. a	198. b	199. b	200. b
201. b	202. b	203. a							

ANSWER KEY

Chapter 5

1. b	2. a	3. b	4. a	5. b	6. b	7. b	8. a	9. b	10. b
11. a	12. a	13. b	14. b	15. b	16. b	17. a	18. a	19. b	20. b
21. b	22. b	23. a	24. b	25. b	26. b	27. b	28. a	29. b	30. b
31. b	32. b	33. a	34. a	35. a	36. a	37. a	38. a	39. a	40. b
41. b	42. a	43. a	44. a	45. b	46. b	47. b	48. a	49. b	50. a
51. b	52. a	53. b	54. b	55. a	56. b	57. b	58. b	59. a	60. b
61. a	62. b	63. a	64. b	65. b	66. b	67. a	68. b	69. a	70. b
71. a	72. a	73. b	74. a	75. b	76. a	77. b	78. a	79. b	80. b
81. a	82. b	83. a	84. b	85. b	86. a	87. b	88. b	89. b	90. a
91. b	92. b	93. b	94. a	95. a	96. b	97. a	98. b	99. b	100. a
101. b	102. b	103. b	104. b	105. a	106. b	107. a	108. a	109. b	110. b
111. a	112. b	113. b	114. b	115. b	116. b	117. b	118. a	119. b	120. a
121. a	122. b	123. a	124. b	125. a	126. a	127. a	128. a	129. b	130. a
131. a	132. b	133. b	134. a	135. a	136. b	137. b	138. a	139. a	140. b
141. a	142. b	143. b	144. a	145. b	146. b	147. b	148. b	149. a	150. b
151. a	152. b	153. b	154. a	155. a	156. b	157. a	158. b	159. a	160. b
161. a	162. b	163. a	164. a	165. b	166. b	167. b	168. b	169. a	170. b
171. b	172. b	173. a	174. a	175. a	176. a	177. a	178. b	179. a	180. a
181. b	182. b	183. b	184. a	185. a	186. a	187. b	188. b	189. b	190. a
191. a	192. a	193. b	194. a	195. b	196. a	197. a	198. b	199. b	200. a
201. b	202. a	203. a							

Chapter 6

1. b	2. b	3. a	4. a	5. b	6. b	7. a	8. b	9. a	10. b
11. a	12. b	13. b	14. a	15. b	16. b	17. a	18. b	19. a	20. a
21. a	22. a	23. b	24. b	25. a	26. a	27. b	28. b	29. b	30. a
31. b	32. b	33. a	34. b	35. a	36. b	37. b	38. b	39. a	40. b
41. b	42. b	43. a	44. a	45. a	46. b	47. a	48. a	49. b	50. a
51. a	52. a	53. a	54. b	55. b	56. b	57. b	58. b	59. b	60. a
61. b	62. a	63. b	64. b	65. b	66. a	67. a	68. b	69. a	70. b
71. b	72. a	73. a	74. a	75. b	76. a	77. b	78. a	79. a	80. b
81. a	82. b	83. b	84. a	85. a	86. a	87. b	88. a	89. a	90. a
91. a	92. a	93. b	94. a	95. a	96. a	97. a	98. a	99. a	100. b
101. a	102. b	103. b	104. a	105. b	106. a	107. a	108. a	109. b	110. b
111. b	112. b	113. a	114. a	115. b	116. a	117. b	118. b	119. a	120. b
121. b	122. a	123. a	124. b	125. a	126. b	127. a	128. b	129. b	130. b
131. b	132. b	133. a	134. a	135. a	136. b	137. b	138. b	139. a	140. b
141. a	142. b	143. a	144. b	145. a	146. a	147. a	148. b	149. b	150. a
151. a	152. a	153. a	154. b	155. a	156. a	157. a	158. a	159. a	160. a
161. b	162. a	163. a	164. a	165. b	166. b	167. b	168. a	169. a	170. a
171. b	172. a	173. a	174. b	175. a	176. a	177. b	178. a	179. b	180. b
181. b	182. a	183. b	184. b	185. a	186. a	187. a	188. a	189. b	190. a
191. b	192. b	193. a	194. b	195. a	196. b	197. a	198. b	199. b	200. b
201. a	202. b	203. b	204. b	205. b	206. b	207. b	208. a		

Chapter 7

1. b	2. a	3. b	4. a	5. b	6. b	7. b	8. a	9. a	10. b
11. b	12. a	13. b	14. a	15. a	16. a	17. a	18. b	19. b	20. b
21. a	22. b	23. a	24. b	25. b	26. a	27. a	28. a	29. a	30. b
31. a	32. a	33. b	34. a	35. b	36. b	37. a	38. a	39. b	40. a
41. a	42. b	43. a	44. b	45. a	46. a	47. b	48. b	49. b	50. a
51. a	52. b	53. a	54. a	55. a	56. b	57. b	58. b	59. a	60. a
61. a	62. b	63. b	64. a	65. b	66. b	67. a	68. a	69. a	70. a
71. b	72. a	73. b	74. b	75. b	76. a	77. b	78. b	79. a	80. a
81. b	82. a	83. b	84. b	85. b	86. b	87. b	88. a		

Chapter 8

1. b	2. a	3. b	4. b	5. b	6. a	7. a	8. a	9. b	10. a
11. b	12. b	13. a	14. a	15. b	16. a	17. a	18. b	19. a	20. a
21. a	22. b	23. b	24. a	25. a	26. a	27. a	28. a	29. a	30. b
31. b	32. b	33. a	34. a	35. b	36. a	37. a	38. b	39. b	40. b
41. b	42. a	43. a	44. b	45. b	46. b	47. a	48. b	49. b	50. b
51. a	52. a	53. b	54. a	55. b	56. a	57. a	58. b	59. b	60. b
61. a	62. b	63. b	64. a	65. a	66. b	67. a	68. a	69. a	70. b
71. a	72. b	73. b	74. b	75. b	76. b	77. b	78. b	79. a	80. a
81. a	82. a	83. a	84. a	85. b	86. b	87. a	88. b	89. a	90. b
91. b	92. b	93. b	94. a	95. b	96. a	97. b	98. a	99. b	100. a
101. b	102. a	103. a	104. a	105. a	106. a	107. b	108. a	109. b	110. a
111. a	112. b	113. a	114. a	115. b	116. a	117. b	118. b	119. b	120. a
121. b	122. b	123. b	124. b	125. b	126. b	127. a	128. a	129. b	130. b
131. a	132. b	133. a	134. a	135. a	136. b	137. a	138. a	139. b	140. a
141. b	142. a	143. b	144. b	145. b	146. a	147. a	148. b	149. a	150. a
151. a	152. b	153. a	154. a	155. b	156. b	157. b	158. a	159. a	160. b
161. b	162. a	163. b	164. a	165. a	166. a	167. b	168. a	169. a	170. a
171. b	172. b	173. a	174. a	175. b	176. a	177. a	178. a	179. a	180. a
181. b	182. a	183. a	184. a	185. a	186. a	187. b	188. b	189. a	190. a
191. a	192. a	193. b	194. b	195. a	196. b	197. b	198. a	199. a	200. a
201. b	202. a	203. a	204. b	205. a	206. a	207. b	208. b	209. a	210. a
211. b	212. a	213. a	214. a	215. a	216. a	217. a	218. b	219. a	220. a
221. b	222. b	223. a	224. a	225. a	226. a	227. b	228. b	229. a	230. a
231. a	232. b	233. b	234. b	235. b	236. b	237. a	238. a	239. b	240. a
241. a	242. b	243. a	244. b	245. a	246. b	247. b	248. b	249. b	250. a

www.ingramcontent.com/pod-product-compliance
Lightning Source LLC
Chambersburg PA
CBHW082204230426
43672CB00015B/2899